Teaching Fiction in Schools

ALSO BY SYDNEY BOLT
The Right Response
Sex and Strife (ed.)
Turning-Points (with Phil Mansell)
Compass (with John Jean Lewis and Phil Mansell)
Twentieth Century Love Poetry (ed.)

TEACHING FICTION IN SCHOOLS

SYDNEY BOLT and ROGER GARD

HUTCHINSON EDUCATIONAL

HUTCHINSON EDUCATIONAL LTD
178–202 Great Portland Street, London W1N 6AQ

London Melbourne Sydney
Auckland Johannesburg Cape Town
and agencies throughout the world

First published 1970

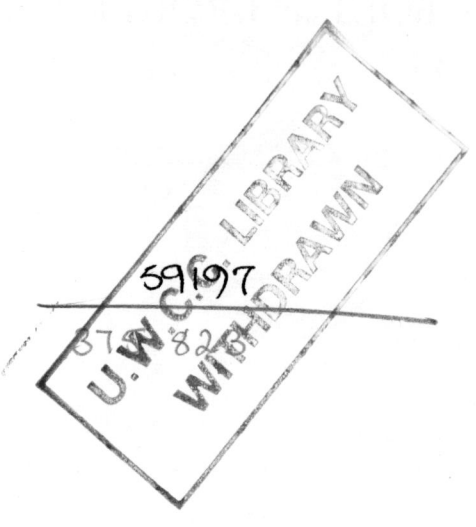

© Sydney Bolt and Roger Gard 1970

*This book has been set in Baskerville type, printed in Great Britain
on smooth wove paper by Anchor Press, and
bound by Wm. Brendon, both of Tiptree, Essex*

ISBN 0 09 105440 0

ACKNOWLEDGEMENTS

The authors and publishers gratefully acknowledge the following for permission to reproduce copyright material:

Messrs Batsford for extracts from *Topics in English* by Geoffrey Summerfield, Messrs Heinemann Educational for extracts from *Teaching English* by J. H. Walsh, Messrs Chatto & Windus for extracts from *The Disappearing Dais* by Frank Whitehead

The material on pages 18 to 21 first appeared in *English in Education* Volume 3, Number 2. Chapters 4 and 5 first appeared in *The Use of English* Volume 20, Numbers 3 and 4 respectively.

The authors would also like to thank publishers of all the books discussed in Chapters 3 to 11.

CONTENTS

1	The Infant Johnson	11
2	Classroom Methods	27
3	A Bear Called Paddington	39
4	The Tower by the Sea	48
5	Dawn Wind	53
6	Treasure Island	59
7	Huckleberry Finn	71
8	Great Expectations	80
9	Pride and Prejudice	97
10	Daughters of the Vicar	111
11	On Being 'With It'	125
12	Ends	148
	Index	155

To our children

I

THE INFANT JOHNSON

WHEN does a child become capable of criticism? This question may seem scarcely worth asking. We all know that infants are among the most critical of mankind, as also at times the most appreciative. Moreover they are notorious for the candour with which they sometimes explain their likes and dislikes.

It is equally unquestionable that children enjoy stories. If, however, our opening question were rephrased, 'When does a child become capable of *literary* criticism?', the answer of many educationalists would seem to be 'not until after O-Level'. For, in current enlightened educational thought, comprehension is regarded as essential and enjoyment as desirable, but criticism is not regarded at all.

Let us consider three recent, representative, and sympathetic books by expert teachers and ask them the question, 'Can a child be, in any sense important to him or her, a literary critic?'. The books we have chosen are *Topics in English* by Geoffrey Summerfield (1965), *Teaching English* by J. H. Walsh (1965) and *The Disappearing Dais* by Frank Whitehead (1966). In our final chapter we shall consider even more recent thought.

Enquiry shows immediately two areas of general agreement, which may at first appear to conflict with one another. (1) That adult teachers know very well that some literature is good, some less good, and some bad—'It [*Moonfleet*] is a better book than *Treasure Island*, I think', says Mr Walsh, typically. (2) That it is not part of the teacher's task to encourage such judgements, or any considerations leading to them, in children. Actually there is no conflict here. First because, in spite of the title and the tendency of Mr Whitehead's excellent book, it is true that experience, and, we trust, education, develop judgement. And because, more importantly, these writers are chiefly, or even exclusively, concerned with the various techniques by which we may bring children to *understand* what they read.

Mr Summerfield occupies a somewhat special territory. He suggests that a fruitful technique in teaching English may be the flexible use of 'Projects' centred around 'Topics' like Predators, the Sea, Horses and Donkeys, Red Indians, War, etc. About these, tactfully handled, pupils are to read, write, talk, imagine, and research. This seems to us an interesting scheme, but one that involves literature only peripherally. Although Mr Summerfield remarks, somewhat in passing and with no ambiguous intent, that 'we should be prepared to let literature *be*, rather than reduce it to the subsidiary role of a stimulus', he also holds (as indeed do we) that 'we presumably understand the novel or short story better than our pupils'. In practice the suggested Projects which occupy most of his book recommend works of art (among many other works) as either stimuli or possible sources of information. For the Topic Australia, 'material suitable for reading aloud by the teacher' includes extracts from two novels by Patrick White and from *Kangaroo*; in that on Fire and Flame the 'Extended Reading' of the pupil includes *The History of Mr Polly*, *Old Saint Paul's*, and *Fahrenheit 451*—and so on. But here the questions must intrude: what of the prior ability of the pupil to understand these works—or to discriminate amongst or within them? Not everything can go under the flexibility blanket.

However, as we have said, other educationalists are very strong indeed on the first of these questions. We trust that the reader will pardon a mosaic of quotation from Mr Walsh and Mr Whitehead, in order that he may savour the general tone on this topic:

> ... the most valuable of all tests of reading is ... the kind of test which sets out to teach in the actual process of testing, and which aims at transforming a superficial reading into a thoughtful one. Here, the teacher is not only trying to find out how deep understanding has gone—he is also trying to deepen it further ... (Walsh).
>
> This method involves, first, a series of readings ... each from a different viewpoint: a reading for the story, a reading for the plot, a reading for the theme or themes, and a reading for the function of the characters (these readings more or less cover the *contents* of the novel); and subsequently, if the pupils are equal to it, readings for the narrative method and the method of presenting the characters ... [these are not necessarily] 'readings from cover to cover', but rather selective surveys concentrated on those matters which for the immediate purpose are relevant. With these readings goes the preparation of a series of reference-lists or 'indexes' ... (Walsh).
>
> ... they [intelligent 12-year-olds] can ... read such books as *Jim Davis* on their own with sufficient understanding to give real enjoyment (Whitehead).
>
> I have already stressed that an overriding aim in reading lessons at this [first form] stage must be to foster an attentive absorption in the content of what is read. ... Can the teacher do more than this? I am convinced that he both can and should—by a limited amount of questioning of a kind which leads the children further 'inside the story'.... Such questions are properly conceived not as tests of understanding, but as aids to understanding; they are designed to draw attention to important aspects of mean-

ing which may have been overlooked or misunderstood, and thereby to help pupils build up for themselves a fuller and more vivid imaginative re-creation of the *author's* experience. (Whitehead, our italics)

> ... it must be remembered that to read with full understanding is an ideal which is seldom if ever attained even by the educated adult; as far as children are concerned, it is a goal which we have to lead them towards gradually. (Whitehead)

Clearly the question of understanding—and that in no narrow 'comprehension' sense—is crucial to the experienced teacher. It rightly claims priority. On the other hand, what is it? *Whose* understanding is it? For what purpose is it desired? Here we feel the formulations of our authors to be less adequate:

> ... one of the functions of literature, in any scheme, will be to exemplify those virtues [in writing] that one is concerned to promote. (Summerfield)

> [a novel should be] a source of pleasure or ... a means of enlivening the mind. (Walsh)

> What do we want of an examination novel, then? ... We want it to give pleasure to the children who read it; we want it to give them an imaginative pre-experience of some of the complexities of actual living; and we want it to be challenging enough to deserve the close study we customarily bestow on it. ... Any proper study of a novel should be something undertaken by teacher and children working together; it should be a process of 'guided reading'; and provided the novel gives scope for that, and the 'guided reading' brings enjoyment and a little increase of maturity, the choice will be the right one. (Walsh)

The Infant Johnson

... to foster an attentive absorption in what is read. (Whitehead)

A children's story, like an adult novel, should be read for the sake of the emotional and imaginative satisfaction it brings; this is the only motive for reading it which the wise teacher will think it worth his while to foster. (Whitehead)

It is ... important that the results of ... further acquaintance (with a passage singled out for attention in class) should be unmistakably rewarding, so that the children themselves feel that the closer attention they have given to the text has increased the enjoyment and satisfaction they have gained from it. (Whitehead)

After the primary end of understanding we are thus offered only the much vaguer ones of satisfaction, enjoyment, preparation for life's famous complexities, and, occasionally, 'insight'. For this one cannot blame our authors: they are rightly concerned with better *methods* of teaching. But what we do find unsatisfying is that, with this practical insistence that children have to be led to understand, there goes a practical failure to recognise that understanding *involves* criticism, even if that criticism is, from the professional point of view, poor. No attention is paid to the child's *judgement* of literature and his reasons for it, as opposed to the (admittedly pressing) questions of boredom, seduction by 'mass media', alienation, bad home background, and so forth. May it not sometimes be the case that, for example, boredom in class is not a reaction to the teaching method but an uncalled for act of literary criticism? Mr Walsh deals with such a point by—with no malicious intent—ridiculing it:

Apart from the subject-matter, what else can we profitably study? The 'art of the novelist' perhaps? Hardly yet; not in general; nor indeed, perhaps, for many a long day.

and:

> ... what about the novelist's manner, the 'way in which it is done', the 'art of the novelist'? Are such studies beyond fifteen-year-old children? In any great detail I think they are ...

The Jamesian vocabulary does its own work. The highfalutin' phrases carry the day. And we can return to 'understanding'. Mr Whitehead, on the other hand, confronts the problem more directly—and in phrases which would seem to make our present enterprise unnecessary:

> No one can be said to have fully mastered the art of reading until he is able not only to take in the meaning of what he reads but also to assess its worth. To consider how much credence we can give to what we read, to estimate its value for us, to decide how much importance to attach to it—are we not bound to admit that 'reading' in its fullest sense must necessarily include these elements within it?

But the word 'credence' gives us the clue to the disappointment that follows. For all Mr Whitehead does with his bold question is to boldly recommend that we should teach discrimination in or against 'that trivialisation which is the hallmark of all popular newspapers and television programmes today' (is this so sweepingly true?), and then to conclude that 'The plain fact is that at present the overwhelming majority of our children leave school before they are mature enough to profit from this kind of training' and that:

> I have no doubt at all that the later years of adolescence form the most fruitful period for this introduction to critical reading. At earlier stages it is seldom profitable to raise questions of value (overtly at any rate) partly because the adult and childish standpoint are too far apart

to offer much common ground, and partly because children's own values and judgements are in any case shifting and changing so rapidly as they grow up.

We are back where we started—'after O-Level'—or perhaps, even more restrictingly, 'at A-Level Eng. Lit.'. When it comes to teaching English in further education, while Sydney Bolt (in *The Right Response*, 1966) accepts fiction as his basic material, the chief use he puts it to ignores the distinction between imaginative literature and reporting. His central aim is to involve his students in a complex and coherent situation, in order to stimulate, in judging the issues which it raises, a complex and coherent use of language. The story is welcomed into the classroom merely because it presents all the relevant aspects of a situation which might occur in actual fact. Stories are to be used in exactly the same way that war games are used in military training, or case studies in the training of business executives, the only difference being that whereas war games and case studies develop operative skills, imaginative literature develops linguistic skills.

In fact all these approaches to fiction in the classroom are well calculated to exercise various skills connected with speaking and listening, reading and writing. Oddly enough, however, none of them is calculated to develop skill in reading fiction *as such*. The purposes of all of them would be served equally well by R. M. Ballantyne's story *The Coral Island* and by Arthur Grimble's reminiscences *A Pattern of Islands*, for, while the element of imagination may be desired in the work of the pupil, it is not essential in that of the author. The experience of reading a factual report is, however, very different from that of reading fiction. If we tell you, as a fact, quite simply that a man fell over a two-hundred-foot cliff and escaped unhurt you will be interested, but you will not be interested if we tell you the same thing, quite simply, as a story.

Somebody who reads a story, or listens to one, expects a

special kind of interest, a special kind of satisfaction. What is more, he regards these expectations as legitimate, so that if they are disappointed he has grounds for a complaint which he would never make against a factual report, as for example that somebody's behaviour in it was arbitrary, or that it failed to follow up issues which it had touched upon, or that it stopped without coming to a conclusion. Children do not, of course, customarily raise such objections, but they nevertheless feel them, and the task of a teacher of critical reading is to develop their awareness of such feelings by inducing their expression, or, conversely, the expression of corresponding satisfactions.

As an example of criticism at the level of early childhood, let us consider a small boy's progressive responses to the story of *Goldilocks*. He is told that a little girl by that name went for a walk one morning in the forest. Already he responds in a way which is appropriate only to fiction. For example, unless he wants to amuse himself by annoying the story-teller, he will not ask, 'Which forest?'. He knows that the phrase 'the forest' has a meaning of its own in stories. More significantly, he feels certain doubts. For one thing, he understands that his sympathetic interest in a little girl is being taken for granted—a little girl as such—and feels a suspicion he would not feel at all if he were told that his little cousin Janet had gone for a similar walk the other day. The information that this little girl answers to the name of Goldilocks increases this suspicion, because answering to a name in fiction is a very different thing from answering to a name in fact. The heroine is next seized by violent hunger, upon which, as he infers that either she is very greedy or else has carelessly gone out without eating her breakfast, the listener's doubts multiply.

So far, however, they are only doubts. Criticism begins when Goldilocks breaks into a strange and empty house, because here the story touches upon an issue without taking account of it. It is true that at this point the story-teller pauses to comment that Goldilocks was naughty to do what

The Infant Johnson

she did. The comment, however, is irrelevant from the listener's point of view. His overwhelming sense is one of rashness. The imbecile heroine, on the other hand, betrays no signs of anxiety. She is still obsessed by the thought of food. But at least the listener is interested now. A catastrophe is imminent.

The catastrophe becomes inevitable when the heroine, still fatuously oblivious of her danger, eats someone else's porridge and then, instead of escaping while she has the chance, breaks a chair and then falls asleep. Her trapped condition, it should be noted, is completed by the circumstance that she is asleep in an upstairs bedroom, so that even if she woke up when the owners of the house returned she could not run for it. The listener's interest is now centred upon the impending confrontation. He cannot imagine what form it is likely to take. The owners of the house are not parents, relatives, or neighbours. Have they the right to punish? If they have not, are they likely, quite naturally, to take revenge? But is it possible for adults to attack a child? Will they perhaps send for the police, and, if so, what would that involve?

At this point, precisely when interest is focussed upon them, the owners of the house return. The story is going well, and as it *is* a story the statement that they are bears and not humans does not spoil it. The listener's sophisticated realisation that it is going to be one of *those* stories does not diminish his interest. After all, the tale of *Little Red Riding Hood* is something to be taken seriously. And the fact that they are bears maintains the suspense. Unlike wolves, bears have an extensive repertoire of behaviour, ranging from the savage grizzly to the friendly teddy. What kind of bears are these?

The story now proceeds in a set form which the listener recognises—from stories like *Red Riding Hood* or even from the game of 'This Little Pig Went to Market'—as conducive to a sudden climax. A verbal pattern is repeated over and over again to be finally and suddenly broken by an action. What form the promised action will take remains excitingly unpredictable, because the manner in which the bears in turn announce their discoveries that somebody has been eating their porridge, sitting on their chairs, and sleeping in their beds, although dramatised, reveals no more than their age and sex. The gruffness of the male is neutralised by the mildness of his mate and the meekness of their offspring. There is no knowing what they will do when they find Goldilocks. One discovery follows another, but their attitude remains inscrutable.

Unfortunately it remains inscrutable to the end. Goldilocks jumps out of the window and runs home before they can do anything at all. The all-important question remains unanswered. The bears do not even say what they would have done to her if they had caught her. The story has opened a door only to close it without going through, leaving the little boy to clinch his disappointment in the reflection that if Goldilocks had really jumped out of an upstairs window she could not have proceeded to run off home because she would have broken her leg at the very least.

He makes this reflection, of course, not because he is a stickler for realism, but because he knows when he has been cheated. The story has ended without coming to a conclusion: the confrontation it has been building up to fails to materialise. If the heroine had only given the bears time to say, 'You ate our porridge so now we're going to eat *you*', it would have been perfectly in order for her to jump out of the window, and the listener would have made no realistic objections. All he wants is for the bears to show their hand. He does not require practical advice on how to deal with bears.

Nor does he require to be told in so many words whether Goldilocks had done wrong. It is true that he wants her trespass to be illuminated, but the illumination must be part of the story. What Goldilocks did can only be illuminated by giving her misdeeds some definite consequence. For this reason, although it involves the idea of punishment, Southey's moralising conclusion would not satisfy our listener any better than the one he has heard. (In Southey's version the intruder is not a little girl but 'a little old Woman'.)

> Now the window was open, because the Bears, like good, tidy Bears as they were, always opened their bed-chamber window when they got up in the morning. Out the little old Woman jumped; and whether she broke her neck in the fall; or ran into the wood and was lost there; or found her way out of the wood, and was taken up by the constable and sent to the House of Correction for a vagrant as she was, I cannot tell. But the Three Bears never saw anything more of her.

There is clearly no hope for the trespasser, but equally clearly her plight would have been just as desperate if she had never broken into the bears' house at all. These endings have nothing to do with the bears, and therefore none of them will do.

Another defect of this conclusion is its multiplicity. Because various endings are offered as alternatives they are all optional, whereas the propriety of a story's ending lies in its necessity. A satisfactory ending might be that the bears ordered Goldilocks to remake the beds, repair the chair, and prepare fresh porridge; or that they kept her upstairs until her parents came to deal with her; or even that they invited her to stay and play with the baby bear. Any one of these endings would do, because they all involve Goldilocks in a relationship with the victims of her intrusion. It would never do, however, to say that the bears did one or another of these things and invite the listener to take his pick. Unlike an algebraic equation, a story can have only one right solution.

The foregoing account of a child's experience of a story raises fundamental critical questions, but what these are, and what a teacher ought to do about them, is not yet under discussion. At this stage the relevant point is that the child does not merely have the experience of understanding the events narrated. He also has the experience of the story as a story, so that when it is ended, while one reaction may be, 'What a silly girl!', another may be, 'I liked it when the big bear said: "Somebody has been eating my porridge!"' The current trend in English teaching is to concentrate on the first kind of reaction. Our contention is that the second kind of reaction deserves no less attention.

Of course, the first kind of reaction cannot be ignored. Taken by itself, the second kind of reaction may be critically valueless. When asked why he liked it when the big bear spoke, the listener might, for example, reply, 'Because he sounded like Louis Armstrong'. In that case, his response would be irrelevant to the story. What is required is not an expression of everything which crossed the listener's mind, but an expression of his reaction to the unfolding tale. Teachers who take care to confirm that their pupils are following the story, that they realise what is going on in it, are surely right to do so. Our suggestion is merely that if this is all that they do, they are neglecting the potential value of what they confirm.

Mr Walsh, for example, offers a series of questions designed to confirm that a reader has followed what is going on in Chapter VIII of *Treasure Island*. In this chapter, prior to the sailing of the *Hispaniola*, Jim Hawkins notices Black Dog, a pirate whom he had previously seen in the company of Pew, convivially seated in Long John Silver's inn at Bristol. Thanks to Silver's handling of the situation, Black Dog makes a get-away and yet Jim fails to put two and two together. With his battery of questions, however, Mr Walsh ensures that his pupils make good Jim's omission and do add things up. e.g.

Q. When he (Silver) addresses Jim as 'our cabin-boy' he speaks *quite loud*. Why does he speak loudly?
A. To warn Black Dog to leave the inn before Jim sees him.
Q. On page 66, Silver enquires, 'Who did you say he

The Infant Johnson

was? Black what?' Why does he make out that he has not caught Black Dog's name?
A. He does not want Jim to think that Black Dog is one of his (Silver's) friends.

These questions ensure that the pupil understands what Jim sees more fully than Jim understands it. But in doing this, they also ensure that the pupil's experience of reading the book has been transformed, because up to this point the pupil has simply shared Jim's point of view. Now, however, he sees not only through Jim's eyes but also round Jim. The point of view is invested with irony. Mr Walsh does *not*, however, suggest any question to confirm that his pupil has registered this transformation. He thus neglects a significant opportunity.

Even more important is the fact that, despite his gullibility at this point, Jim does not forfeit the reader's sympathy. Perhaps this fact does not require confirmation by a question, but the case is different when we return to the listener who remarks that Goldilocks was a silly little girl. It is surely worth asking him, 'Then did you want the bears to hurt her?', for this would direct his attention to a richness in his reaction to the story of which he might otherwise remain unconscious. The audience which has just witnessed Lear's division of his kingdom might well remark, 'What a silly old man!', but they would make this remark in a very different spirit from that of Goneril's, 'You see how full of changes his age is'. The most serious omission involved in the approach to a story which stops short at comprehension of the plot is that it neglects to chart the flow of the reader's sympathies with the characters involved in it.

Although he finds it necessary to direct pupils to maintain dossiers on the characters in 'examination novels', Mr Walsh deprecates close examination of characters in the class reader.

The most we want the children to do is to observe those

things about the characters which affect the development of the plot and its outcome; we want them to see the characters in relation to the story, and not to 'reconstruct' them as if they were living persons.

The warning contained in the second half of this sentence is salutary. But seeing 'the characters in relation to the story' means much more than observing those things about them 'which affect the development of the plot'. The plot is not by any means the whole story. The plot would be lifeless if the reader did not feel something for the characters involved in it, and it is a deeply interesting task to promote full consciousness of what that something is.

We hope that the direction of our argument is now clear. We assert that the 'understanding' of fiction is *in fact* inseparable from the criticism (perhaps 'evaluation' is a clearer word) of what is understood. This ought to be a commonplace, and probably is outside educational textbooks. We conclude therefore that this evaluation needs the guidance of the teacher in exactly the *same* degree as does the understanding. And we believe that a key to the process is the elicitation of the pupil's stance towards, his amount of sympathy with, characters and situations as the fiction progresses. This applies equally to all ages and all levels of ability.

Discussion of the point that most obviously arises from this argument—that of conflicting or shifting sympathies— we shall postpone to specific treatments of novels and stories in the ensuing chapters. But for the present two items remain outstanding. One is a practical point, the other theoretical. The practical point is, paradoxically, the least important. It is that if we are correct in asserting that understanding is in fact not separable from evaluation, then it should follow that most teachers will have found this out, whatever they *think* about it. The enlightened teacher will have no motive, and almost certainly no desire, to suppress the fact. What point, then, have our platitudes? There are several answers: (1) That not all teachers are enlightened; (2) that even those that are appear to be ill led in *theory*, and in recommendation as to practice, by the educational thinkers we have reviewed, and, (3) that consequently they may consider their pupils' 'free' discussion of their sympathies, etc., as a kind of creative holiday, a smoke-break after the serious work of understanding has been accomplished. (4) That if all teachers actually already followed what we now, superfluously, recommend, we would be at least reinforcing a process which is condemned or ignored by advanced thinkers in the field. (5) That we hope in the ensuing chapters to provide helpful (although not, of course, definitive) models of procedure.

The second item is more fundamental. It concerns the nature of fiction. If all one is doing in teaching the novel or story is to make people understand what did not in fact take place, then one is pursuing a profitless activity. Fiction is not history, but neither is it (in this sense) lies. We have therefore to consider, even in the classroom, what it is. Thus: since a fact in fiction is untrue its importance can only be assessed in terms of what it does to an audience, whether of children or of adults. The modern traditional question 'Do they understand?' ought therefore to be replaced by 'How should they understand this, about this character, at this moment . . . etc.?'. Writers are known to manipulate their effects with some care, and to be generally indifferent to historical truth as such. The job of the teacher must be to help the class to discover the *kind* of truth which is embodied in fiction, and he can only do this by drawing attention to its effects on them. By encouraging, that is, a critical reading, at whatever level is, in some way or other, appropriate. The adult paraphernalia of 'point of view', 'narrative structure', 'irony', etc., etc., would of course be oppressive if poured on to a child's (or indeed an undergraduate's) head as terms implying *knowledge*. They would indeed have far worse effects than the irrelevance mentioned by Mr Walsh. But, once realise that they, and their more rudimentary equivalents, are useful only as a necessary (and possibly misleading) shorthand for effects already experienced, and the situation is transformed. Seeing round Jim Hawkins in Chapter VIII of *Treasure Island* involves a shift in our 'point of view'. But there is absolutely no need to mention this discreditable fact, so long as we are able to make the pupil aware that his response to Jim—his trust and sympathy—is being guided by Stevenson into a slightly different, but also fruitful, channel. To repeat: if this was not the case then it could not matter less what happens in Silver's Inn, since it never happened.

In support of our argument we hope that it will not seem pretentious to quote (yet again) some of the best passages in *Lady Chatterley's Lover*:

> It is the way our sympathy flows and recoils that really determines our lives. And here lies the vast importance of the novel, properly handled. It can inform and lead into new places the flow of our sympathetic consciousness, and it can lead our sympathy away in recoil from things gone dead.

We are suggesting that there is no justification for assuming that recognition of this 'vast importance' can be reserved until after O-Level; and that the purpose of teaching the novel would be best served by making the pupil as fully as possible aware of the flow of his sympathetic consciousness. It is really a matter of cultivating what is already there.

2

CLASSROOM METHODS

IF ITS unique educational value is to be realised, fiction must be read critically. As we have said, this means that it must not be read as fact. When we are concerned with small children, this requirement may seem a tall order. It almost seems as if we were stipulating that they must read without enjoyment. The earliest, and still the most fundamental, impulse to continue listening to a tale is the desire to know what happens next, and the tale can hardly engage that kind of curiosity unless, in some way, we regard it as true. Curiosity, after all, is a desire to *know*, and knowledge concerns facts. If we inform you that this book is the work of two baboons who wear polka-dotted bow ties, assuming you guess that we are lying, you will not be curious to know what colour the dots are. But the first time you read *Pride and Prejudice*, as you approached the end, you were probably possessed by a burning curiosity to know whether the quite fictitious Mr D'Arcy was going to repeat his proposal of marriage to the equally fictitious Elizabeth Bennet. It seems as if what distinguishes imaginative literature from other forms of untruth lies precisely in the fact that it *can* be the object of curiosity.

Curiosity, however, is the least permanent form of suspense. In its own fulfilment, it destroys itself. The question where flies go in the wintertime can never engage your curiosity again, once you have ascertained the answer. Similarly, when you know what is going to happen, you cannot also enjoy a desire to know. Curiosity, however, is not the only form of suspense. There is another form, entirely different, which is not merely proof against foreknowledge but may even be enhanced by it. You can see what is coming, and yet remain in a state of suspense—*this* sort of suspense—over its arrival. This anticipatory form of suspense is not peculiar to fiction. Certain actual events of a doom-laden kind also exercise it: these are the events which quickly become legendary, like The Last Days of Hitler, or The Day Father Decided to Do It Himself. But this capacity to survive repetition is more characteristic of fiction—and not only fiction designed for the highly trained audiences of Greek tragedy. On the contrary, the old old story which we ask to be told again is often a children's tale, and the children, manifesting an admirable attention to detail, insist that the repetition must be textually accurate.

Suspense of this kind has its source in the story's activation of some of the reader's deepest concerns. The suspense in *Pride and Prejudice* is a case in point. It is not curiosity, but anticipation. Even on the first reading, the reader knows from the start that Elizabeth and Mr D'Arcy are meant for each other and are going to get each other. Of course, the cognitive status of such knowledge can be questioned. There is, however, no doubt as to the status of the reader's knowledge on this point in the course of his next reading, but once again the same suspense arises. What kind of anxiety is this? It has nothing to do with the characters, because we know they will come to no harm. It has something to do with more general possibilities which concern us deeply, as for example the possibility that the reserves and delicacies which make permanent intimacy—marriage, in a word—possible, may also operate to keep people apart. The pleasures of suspense, therefore, do not depend on treating a tale as if all its incidents were true, but rather upon realising their deepest interest.

Classroom Methods

For this reason, the method by which fiction should be taught in schools is the leisurely one of passing and realising, described by Coleridge in *Biographia Literaria* (Chapter XIV).

> The reader should be carried forward, not merely or chiefly by the mechanical interest of curiosity, or by a restless desire to arrive at the final solution; but by the pleasurable activity of mind excited by the attractions of the journey itself. Like the motion of the serpent, which the Egyptians made the emblem of intellectual power, or like the path of sound through the air, at every step he pauses and half recedes, and from the retrogressive movement collects the force which again carries him onwards.

The function of the teacher is to serve as a guide on such a journey, making sure that the travellers in his charge enjoy, as far as they are capable, 'the attractions of the journey itself'. There is no one set method to ensure that he will succeed in this task. In part his task will vary with the journey. If he is conducting them across a range of mountains, clearly he will not direct their attention in the same direction as he would upon a river cruise. Accordingly, instead of erecting some all-purpose critical apparatus, in the following pages we have examined a series of different novels and stories suitable for readers of different ages, showing in each case what the principal features of interest are. But even with regard to each particular journey, it is still not possible to lay down fixed instructions for the guide —as anybody will agree who has had his interest in some marvel destroyed by a guide operating under fixed instructions, whether in a classroom or in a château on the Loire. To continue our metaphor, if a mountain journey is in hand the guide will have little need to direct his clients' attention to the wildflowers, if they are botanists: indeed, they may even direct *his* attention to details which he has ignored on earlier journeys over the same terrain. On the other hand, they may require more encouragement than his clients usually do to take extensive views. Accordingly, even in our treatment of individual stories, we have not attempted to lay down a foolproof treatment. There is no set of questions, however tedious, complete enough to guide the attention of every possible reader, and none, however tenuous, which will not prove redundant in the individual case.

Nevertheless, it may be profitable to demonstrate what an exhaustive battery of critical questions would be like, in order to indicate the various aspects of a work of fiction which may, or may not, require attention according to the capacity of the reader. For this purpose, we will now examine *Goldilocks* again, this time from the point of view of a teacher concerned to sharpen his pupils' awareness of the story. Our reasons for choosing this story are, first, that the various lines of questioning can be related to the response to the story already described; second, that the story is short enough for an exhaustive treatment not to be too long; third, and most important of all, that an exhaustive treatment is so obviously inappropriate that no reader will imagine that we are advocating its application to this or any other story. The object of the exercise is merely to indicate the different lines of questioning which may, or more probably may not, prove useful.

It should not be, but it nowadays in fact is, necessary to warn the teacher that his pupils are already in possession of all the equipment required to appreciate the story of *Goldilocks*. The warning is necessary because Gradgrind rides again. There are educationalists who feel that the presence of fiction in the classroom can be justified only if it is tied to the facts of life as presented in History, Geography, Science, and other lessons with impeccable credentials. As against this, our contention is simply that imaginative experience has its own special value. It requires no extraordinary preparation in terms of knowledge—and this includes internal knowledge of the self no less than external knowledge of the universe. A story which has no application

Classroom Methods

to one's own case is no less interesting for that. As Wordsworth observes in *The Prelude*, after castigating the 'modern system' of education:

> Oh! give us once again the wishing-cap
> Of Fortunatus, and the invisible coat
> Of Jack the Giant-Killer, Robin Hood,
> And Sabra in the forest with Saint George!
> The child, whose love is here, at least, doth reap
> One precious gain, that he forgets himself.

In our view, therefore, the only support (as distinct from stimulus) which a child's reading may require is a tentative definition of new words, and even here it is surprising how much of the work of definition can be left to the context in many cases. Pupils about to listen to the story of *Goldilocks* certainly do not require the kind of preparation recommended by Robert Whitehead (in *Children's Literature*, 1968), in order 'to generate interest' and 'to build the concepts', namely:

> asking the children to tell *facts* they know or experiences they or others have had with bears;
> discussing a previously read or told story about bears;
> discussing a current local happening that centred upon bears;
> showing a flat or still picture, movie, or other visual aid dealing with bears.

These suggestions all totally ignore the status of fiction as fiction. Three of them provide the children with background information about real bears which could only prove bewildering when they were introduced to bears who lived in a cottage and had porridge for breakfast. The other reminds them of fictitious bears which they have encountered in other stories, as if the world of fiction were continuous. What help would the children derive from remembering Winnie-the-Pooh? But then, what help do they require? They are far more sophisticated than some educationalists give them credit for—and even, it might appear, more sophisticated than some educationalists, in whom the organs of tacit understanding have perhaps atrophied.

One area where the child's tacit understanding is far more solid than the vociferous understanding of some educationalists is the borderland of fact and fiction. A child who has taken great care all morning not to cross the edge of the hearthrug because, in his game, it represents the edge of a precipice, will cross it without hesitation the moment he is informed that lunch is ready. He is aware of the element of 'make' in make-believe, to such an extent that he can even share with others in a regulated, common fantasy—for example, that the people next door are disguised invaders from outer space—and act this fantasy out in company with them in accordance with rules which prevent it from getting out of hand. The imaginative processes of children are conscious procedures, just like the imaginative processes of artists.

They have a highly developed sense of 'entertainment', in that very special and important sense of the word as meaning 'undertaking' which the Chorus in *King Henry the Fifth* uses when he opens Act IV, requesting the audience:

> Now entertain conjecture of a time
> When creeping murmur and the poring dark
> Fills the wide vessel of the universe.

Any story is a 'conjecture'—something thrown together, a composition of various empirical elements—a concoction, in fact, which, unlike reality, is something we are free to take or leave. If we take it, we do so consciously, harbouring or entertaining it in much the same way as we might do a hypothesis, although not for the same reason, because all that can be proved is the intrinsic interest of the entertainment. It has no further consequences.

This act of entertainment is the foundation of any critical

reading. To confirm its presence in connection with *Goldilocks* the teacher might put a question about the location of 'the forest' (see Chapter 1). Or, if the story opens with the words 'Once upon a time', the way this means 'any time you like, or in other words never' could be investigated. Or a question about the acceptability of alternative endings, and particularly the all-important question, 'Which ending is the right one?', could be asked.

The latter question, by insisting on the hypothetical nature of the story, clarifies the reader's detachment from the story. At the same time the idea that an ending can be right or wrong also draws attention to the basic interest of the story, its underlying tension. In the case of *Goldilocks*, as we suggested in Chapter 1, this lies in the evaluation of the seriousness of the heroine's trespass in terms of its consequences, especially the reactions of the offended parties. The right ending is one which portrays the bears' reaction and does not minimise the seriousness of the situation. Because the story as given dodges the issues it raises, many children just forget what happens after the bears discover the girl in bed. The teacher's request for a better ending is a good way to convert this disappointment into criticism. It can be prepared for earlier in the story by questions such as—'Could the story end here?' (asked at the point where Goldilocks falls asleep)—and even 'What do you think is going to happen now?' (asked at the point where the bears arrive). Both the questions help to make the children realise what they *want* to happen, bearing in mind that it is all a fiction and that therefore nobody real, except possibly the reader, is any the worse for an unhappy ending.

Considering questions aimed at making critical detachment conscious led us on to questions aimed at eliciting an awareness of the basic interest of the story. The latter have now similarly led us on to questions which register the way in which the story is going, the kind of thing which is happening and is likely to happen next—what, we have insisted, the reader *wants* to happen next. 'And then what do you suppose happened?', asked at the point where Goldilocks falls asleep, might well, or at least logically, produce the answer, 'She tossed and turned so much she tore the sheets.' Such a development would certainly be in line with the heroine's earlier destructiveness. But the reader has had enough of that, and feels that the ground has now been prepared for something different. The answer accordingly—what he wants to happen, in fact—will more probably be, 'The people who lived in the cottage came home'.

Awareness of the way in which the story is going can, of course, be more a perception of formal elements—'what I call the *shape* of the story', explained a seven-year-old critic who had to invent his own terminology. A child is as capable as anybody else of perceiving that tit is the reverse of tat, that the situation at the end of a fable like *The Fox and the Stork* mirrors the situation with which it starts. The sequence of events in *Goldilocks* follows a pattern which is quickly picked up and anticipated: the bears follow in the intruder's footsteps, and make their discoveries in strict order of precedence—first father, then mother, last of all baby—an order which is also conducive to climax, because in each case it is the baby bear who has suffered most. A child's perception of this pattern could be made more conscious, by simply asking what he expects happened next at any point in this sequence.

At this part of the story formal expectations are so precise that they extend to linguistic detail. Asked, at the point where the bears troop upstairs to their bedroom, what he supposes Father Bear had to say, no child experiences any difficulty in supplying the answer—'Somebody's been sleeping in my bed.' Nor is this question, because it is about words rather than events, any less interesting than the others. The admirable closeness with which children follow the words as well as the action of a story is simply proved by their infallible detection of any alterations or omissions of language when it is repeated. They enjoy adjectives, word-play, similes. Less welcome, but sometimes more necessary,

Classroom Methods

is the examination of phrases whose full implications are not immediately grasped in full.

Even less spontaneous, initially, may be the child's enjoyment of ironical implications. Irony, however, cannot be ignored. It is directly related to the experience of fiction as fiction rather than fact, because it is based on a secret understanding between narrator and listener, writer and reader, whereby they share a joke at the expense of the characters. Since children readily use mimicry as a form of ridicule, the simplest form of irony is easily appreciated. This is what occurs when a character's limitations are presented dramatically. Thus, if after she has eaten the porridge and broken the chair, Goldilocks is made to say, 'I've done so many good deeds this morning, I've earned a little rest upstairs', then a nod is as good as a wink to the alert child critic.

Suppose, however, the irony does not arise from the words spoken by a character, but from words issuing directly from the narrator himself. The child suspects that they are words which the narrator does not really mean. Who is being mocked now? It looks unpleasantly as if, instead of mocking the fictitious heroine for her obtuseness, the narrator is mocking his listener for his. Some way must be found to help the child to understand that irony need not be aggressive, that it can be a game.

When considering a story like *Goldilocks* it is natural to speak of the listener. It is not easy to imagine a story of this kind being read. It has to be told *viva voce*, and all our observations so far have been consistent with this method of narration. The texts we consider in subsequent chapters are, on the other hand, definitely readers, and it is as a reader that we must also consider *Goldilocks*. In many ways the difference is not as great as might be supposed, because if critical reading is required the only way in which to treat a reader in class is to read it aloud. This is not the same as the teacher telling the story, because each pupil must have a copy of the text open in front of him, and follow the live reading on the page. Nevertheless, he is not reading on his own. His reading of the page is reinforced by the teacher's: the emphasis and tone of the teacher's voice bring out structures and implications which might otherwise require excavation. Moreover, the class stays together throughout the reading, instead of splitting up into a horde, migrating through the book, with rapid readers spurring on ahead and slow readers straggling miles behind in the rear. This is essential for critical reading, for criticism is essentially a collaborative enterprise, based on a shared experience. It can, of course, be conducted as a post-mortem, and sometimes has to be, but for young readers it is always best to raise a critical question at a point where its interest is vital, a point in the narrative where the narrative is still unfolding. It is therefore possible only if the readers all reach these points together.

The experience, therefore, is very similar told orally without benefit of text. Nevertheless, the presence of the text does make a crucial difference at certain times, one of which is when irony is in question. It is a text for the teacher, just as it is for the pupil. Although the teacher speaks the words, they are not *his* words. The teacher, therefore, can speculate about what the words mean in company with his pupils, and if irony is involved he stands in the same relation to it as they do.

Let us imagine a version of *Goldilocks* which contains the following passages. (1) At the point where the heroine tastes the porridge: 'Now Goldilocks was so pretty, she knew that nobody could ever be angry with her.' (2) When the bears discover her asleep: 'She looked so pretty, only a wicked person could find fault with her.' The earlier of these additions, by virtue of an ironical use of the word 'knew', operates in a manner similar to that of the transparent irony of Goldilocks saying to herself, 'I've done so many good deeds this morning, etc.' But the word 'knew' is not placed in the mouth of Goldilocks. It is the narrator's own word. Asked what he thought about it, therefore, the reader might well reply that her complacency was justified. But if a similar question is put about the second addition, the pupil will probably answer that the narrator is 'making fun'. A return to the first instance will now probably prompt a similar sense of leg-pull. If it does so, there is no harm in providing the pupil with the word 'irony'. Vocabulary aids perception in this as in other fields of experience—literary or non-literary—and there are few fields of experience where a sense of irony may not come in handy. Needless to say, irony is not a simple function of detachment. Sympathy is no less a factor in its production, and the irony of the example we have offered—a bland confidence that charm will exempt the wrongdoer from the consequences of her misdeeds—hinges on the basic interest of the story, the reader's contradictory sense that consequences are inevitable.

His appreciation of irony therefore depends upon a dialectic of play and earnest in the child's response to the tale. So also do those other elements of his response which we have advised the teacher to elicit by questioning—his anticipation of what will happen next, his appreciation of the formal elements of the narrative, and of the details of linguistic usage. So too, above all other elements of his experience of the story, does the fluctuation of his sympathy with the characters. His interest as a detached spectator wishes Goldilocks into a dangerous situation: his interest as a participant in her vulnerability wishes her safe out of it. Within this framework, the changing course of the narrative also affects the current of his feeling. Before their arrival on the scene, alarm on Goldilocks' account at the damage she is doing is tempered by indignation on behalf of the aggrieved parties. When they do arrive, and are revealed to be bears, this dramatic division of sympathy may be intensified—or, again, sympathy may take a turn entirely for or against the trapped human being.

This element of the experience of fiction, the flow of sympathy, is the most vital of all, and produces the liveliest response of all to those questions which are aimed at its development. And there are other stimuli in addition to questions: for example, messages to the characters as the story proceeds. 'If you had passed by the cottage at this point, what would you have said to Goldilocks?' (Similarly, when a full-length novel is being read with older pupils, the characters can be offered written advice in letters.) Sympathy, or the lack of it, can be further developed by asking the pupil to devise a message not as a spectator, but as a character. 'Imagine you are Goldilocks. You wake up, and hear the bears talking downstairs. There is a telephone by your bed. Who will you ring? What will you say to them?' From this it is a short step to dramatisation. A counter movement, back towards detachment, is the preparation of a scenario for a film of some episode in the story, which has the effect of making the class see each character from the outside, as part of a total effect.

No teacher would want to do half this work with a class reading *Goldilocks*, but upon occasion any of these types of question and lines of approach can help children to read critically. Only tact can tell the difference between those occasions when an instrument of criticism can be helpfully applied and those when its application spells murder. To a large extent this tact depends upon knowledge of the character of the pupil, which only the teacher can supply. The rest depends upon knowledge of the particular character of the story in hand—provision of which is the business of the chapters which follow. We shall assume that teachers will be, or may easily make themselves, familiar with the works we shall discuss.

3

A BEAR CALLED PADDINGTON

ANIMALS gifted with the power of speech are common enough in children's stories. The convention is, however, used with unique sophistication in *A Bear Called Paddington* by Michael Bond. It is not just that Paddington talks, but that he talks only to human beings, and lives in the everyday human world. Puss-in-Boots is his only rival in this respect, but Puss-in-Boots lives in a fairytale world, not in the realistic world in which the Browns discover a bear 'sitting on some kind of a suitcase, and around its neck there was a label with some writing on it. The suitcase was old and battered, and on the side, in large letters, were the words 'WANTED ON VOYAGE.'

Before the bear has exchanged many words with the family, it has established its right to the pronoun 'he', and all the niceties of the convention which is to govern the narrative are well established before the end of the first chapter. In the first place, there are the reactions of the human characters to the appearance of a bear in their midst. The waitress in the station buffet takes special note not, as might be expected, of the surprising fact of his presence there, but only of his unhygienic intention of eating other patrons' left-overs. Similarly the taxi-driver is concerned only, as he might be in the case of a child passenger, at the sticky mess he makes. Above all, the Browns betray no doubts as to the feasibility of living cheek-by-jowl with a bear, but only as to its possible inconveniences. From what these human characters take for granted the reader learns what he too is to take for granted. Similar guidance is provided by what the writer feels called upon to explain and what he does not. Thus, while explanation is provided for the fact that he speaks English, no explanation is provided for the more surprising basic fact that he speaks at all, and while the strangeness of his headgear is occasion for comment, the fact that he should wear a hat at all is not.

The child reader picks up these clues, and accordingly adjusts his view of the world in which the story unfolds. The *critical* child reader does not merely do this: he is also aware of doing it. How is this awareness to be stimulated? A suggested comparison with Puss-in Boots might produce the desired effect, but is more likely to produce unhelpful discussion of these two animals as if they enjoyed an existence independent of the fictions which endow them with the only life they have.

The answer to the problem is surely, as always, to return to the experience of reading and consider how it has been affected by the feature we are trying to bring to light. The effect of a convention is to expand or contract the range of possibility in a story, and the reader's expectations are expanded or contracted accordingly. A child reading *A Bear Called Paddington* can therefore be made aware of the conventions he has accepted by considering such questions as, 'Could Paddington talk to birds and dogs?' (No). 'Would it be bad manners in him to lick his chops and scratch?' (No). 'Would it be bad manners in him to snatch food?' (Yes). These and similar questions make clear the peculiar status of Paddington, how simultaneously like and unlike a real bear he is, and the answer to each one requires justification. 'How do you know?' The reader then realises the significance of the clues which have guided him.

Having established its conventions, what use does the book make of them? How relevant is Paddington's animal status? Might he not just as well have been a child? Several of the stories, especially those towards the end (in chapters 5, 7 and 8), do not withstand this test. In these stories Paddington's motivation is identical with that of any incorrigible coy lord of misrule, such as Richmael Crompton's William, and the adventures into which they plunge him are just of that kind. The fact that he is a bear is relevant only because it confers upon him an immunity from blame. After all, you can't expect from a bear the considered behaviour demanded even of a child. This irresponsibility, however, is quite uncharacteristic of Paddington when we first meet him, and it is necessary therefore, before bringing criticism to bear upon his degeneration, to appraise him in his prime.

When first encountered on Paddington Station, he has many of the characteristics of an adult. Admittedly, the label round his neck reading, 'Please look after this bear', might well have been attached to some infant despatched unprotected on a long journey, but his poise destroys any such effect. When the Browns first approach him he rises to his feet, raises his hat, and inquires, 'Can I help you?' His status is analagous to that of a well-bred youth, not of a child—witness the delicacy with which he touches on the problem of paying for his board and lodging. We are not surprised to learn that he has waited until he was 'old enough' before emigrating from darkest Peru. The mess he makes in the course of eating a cream bun shows that he is not to be completely identified with a well-bred youth, but at the same time it is not due to his being infantile. He asks whether anyone would mind if he stood on the table to eat, before actually doing so, and is in fact constrained to this eccentricity by the need to hold the bun down firmly with one paw. Indeed, he is in the semi-tragic situation of being a well-bred youth in bear's clothing, like the prince who was transformed into a frog, and the courtesy of the Browns is demonstrated by their unspoken and immediate awareness of this special status.

How is a similar awareness to be confirmed in the child reader? The central point, clearly, is Paddington's maturity. This can be readily focussed on by raising the question whether he is a full-grown bear or a baby bear, and, as before, when the reader is asked to justify his answer to this question he is led to discover in the text itself the sources of the impression he has gained from it.

Once Paddington's peculiar plight has been recognised, a major critical question arises—what is its interest as a source of narrative invention? At the end of the first chapter, as the Browns arrive home with Paddington, Judy warns him not to be afraid of Mrs Bird, their housekeeper. Mrs Bird, she informs him, is fierce and apt to grumble, and then proceeds to assure him that he will like her. To this he replies, 'I'm sure I shall like her, if you say so. But will she like me?' His anxiety indicates where, at this stage of the book, its centre of acutest interest lies. Further developments can be expected to depict the comic relations of normal members of a civilised society with a visitor who, despite his innate courtesy, is constitutionally incapable of conforming with all its mores.

Critical appraisal of the experience offered by the ensuing chapters requires that before they are read this expectation should be fully realised, because they meet it only partially. The first chapter contains sufficient evidence that a bear cannot be introduced into human society without causing both embarrassment and extra work. It also establishes the fact that while the Browns are well equipped to weather the embarrassment, they expect others to do the work. The usual kind of comprehension questions, aimed at determining their position in society, will make this adequately clear. Once this has been done, however, further questions are needed to clarify the point of view of the taxi-driver whose coat Paddington smears with cream. In this way, some sympathy may be generated for Mrs Bird, and the occasional ferocity and grumbling which Judy reports of her. What will her attitude be? Will Paddington's tact and decency suffice to mitigate the inconvenience of his intrusion? What, in short, will happen next?

It is important to whet these expectations, because after the first chapter they are legitimate, and a critical reading of the second chapter requires that their disappointment should not be lost sight of in the hilarity occasioned by Paddington's misadventures in the bathroom. His encounter with Mrs Bird results in an immediate knockout victory for the bear. Although the family professes anxiety as to what her reaction will be when they tell her that Paddington is going to stay in the house permanently, the reader does not share their misgivings. It is worth asking, therefore, why, when so much advance emphasis has been given to the housekeeper's grumpiness, she proves so agreeable in the event. This would be a comprehension question, if the answer were that long ago a philanthropic bear had saved her from drowning, or that something about Paddington had reminded her of her dead father. As no such explanation is offered, however, the question is a critical one, like the question, 'Why is there no mint in this mint sauce?' In view of the expectations aroused in him earlier, the reader has grounds for complaint. At this point it is worth fostering the realisation that, because it is not a factual record, a story could always have been otherwise. The question might be put, for example, 'What would *you* have had Mrs Bird do and say, if the children had not cleared up the mess in the bathroom?'

As for the bathroom romp itself, the critical question is, 'Is this the same bear?' Would so considerate a creature have used up all his host's shaving cream? Would an animal so mature have used it to draw maps on the floor? Would a self-reliant bear, who had crossed the Atlantic as a stowaway, lose his head in the bath so completely that he did not think to pull the plug when he wanted to lower the water-level? Most important of all, has the scrape he gets into anything at all to do with his being a bear? Might it not just as easily have been the misdemeanour of a spoilt and stupid five-year-old child? Is he not, indeed, to blame for the mess?

To all these searching questions, of course, the honest answer may well be: 'Who cares? It's funny, and what's more I'd far rather have it than a lot of harrowing stuff about Mrs Bird.' At a point like this, the teacher is in danger of seeming to belittle the pupil's genuine enjoyment of the bathroom farce, prematurely forcing him into the obdurate I-know-what-I-like position. It is enough to bring him to perceive that, although the farce is certainly enjoyable, it does not require Paddington at its centre. After all, *The Merry Wives of Windsor* is an enjoyable comedy, even if the character of Falstaff is wasted in it. The relative weakness of this chapter is apparent enough if it is compared with one of those in which the character of Paddington is *not* wasted.

Of these chapters—namely 3, 4 and 6—the best is the fourth, in which Mrs Brown takes Paddington shopping at Barkbridge's, a fashionable store, to fit him out with a new hat and coat. Here the narrative depends entirely on his being a bear in man's clothing, and the social effect of this oddity. As in the first chapter, the theme is courtesy. Castiglione would surely endorse Paddington's comportment in this piece. The haughty salesman starts by indicating that the Gentleman's Outfitting department is the wrong place to have brought him, and suggests that Mrs Brown should try the bargain basement, where government surplus stock is on sale. (The narrative convention is so well-established that it is actually being played with at this point: nobody would dream of suggesting that a bear requires no clothes at all.) By the time the purchases are complete, however, Paddington has put the salesman completely in his place—indeed, has reduced him to a far lower one—simply by the hauteur of his glance. No snob, however, he has simultaneously given kindly encouragement to Albert, the salesman's downtrodden assistant, with whom he shakes hands on departing, while favouring his superior merely with a crushing stare.

He continues this demonstration of nobility with the *sprezzatura* he proceeds to exhibit before an enormous crowd when having upset the display in Barkridge's show-window he calmly rearranges it in the manner he personally thinks most attractive. These feats demonstrate that he is admirable. That he is also different he demonstrates when, upon being offered anything in the store as a reward, he selects a large jar of marmalade.

Apart from clarification of the point that it is not fear of a bear at large but recognition of a superior spirit which makes the salesman quake before Paddington, no special effort is required for the *comprehension* of this chapter, in the sense of understanding the rationale of events. The teacher who is interested in the experience of his pupils has nevertheless a lot to do. The story has engaged their sympathies and antipathies. The critical question is—how did this come about? Finding an answer to this question will, no doubt, sometimes require attention to the choice of a word. It is not, however, a matter of studying the tricks of the writer's trade. All that is necessary is that the pupils should be asked to account for their experience, to justify, that is, their sympathies and antipathies by reference to narrative details.

Material for adverse criticism which offers valuable insight into the nature of fiction is offered in chapters five, seven and eight. In these Paddington is neither different nor admirable. As regards the first point, it is probably enough to establish that a story about a bear which makes no use of the fact that a bear is what he is, is as wasteful as a story about a giant which makes no use of his size. The second point, however—that Paddington ceases to be admirable—is worth detailed attention. In these stories Paddington shows a regrettable lack of the gentlemanly impulses which characterise his more memorable performances. He is increasingly vainglorious, boastful, and greedy for the limelight. Stranger still, in place of his pristine drive for marmalade we find avarice. In the second chapter, when he shows Judy his carefully polished centavos and tells her that he never spends them, this sounds like the declaration of a collector and a connoisseur. In the fifth chapter, however, we find him driving hard bargains with shop-keepers and trying to make money out of paintings. In the sixth chapter he creates a scene about the price of theatre programmes. In the seventh, the prospect of winning two pounds by building a sand-castle causes him to swoon.

The seventh chapter is merely one more appearance of your-friend-and-mine the irrepressible Paddington, but chapters five and eight have each a specific interest from the critical point of view which does not call for an A-Level in order to be appreciated. Chapter Five has a cheap satirical point, in that the accidental daub of a bear wins first prize as a modern painting. More interesting is its use of suspense, at the meeting where the award is announced. This is described at length, and the reader can tell what the outcome is going to be long before it is presented. His sense of the way the story is going tells him, and increases his enjoyment of the interim. Making the pupil aware of his experience of the story will involve drawing his attention to this feature of it, and the way in which it came about.

The eighth chapter contains a simple example of cheating —including the straining of the story in order to place the reader's sympathies where the author requires them to be, instead of where they would naturally be drawn by the tale. On the occasion of his birthday-party, Paddington gives a display with one of his presents, a conjuring set. He attempts a trick which involves appearing to hammer a watch supplied by a member of the audience. The trick does not work, and the watch is smashed. For this damage, either Paddington is entirely to blame, since he has neglected to rehearse the trick, or else the Browns are also culpable for precipitating the situation. The whole story is, however, twisted to rule out any question of responsibility. This is done by presenting Mr Curry, the victim of the outrage, as a person who deserves no sympathy.

It is easy to show how this is done, because the story is

made completely implausible as a result of the effort. We are given Mr Brown's hostile judgement of Mr Curry—but why should we give any weight to his opinion in view of his inept showing in the previous chapters? We are told that he was unpopular in the neighbourhood. So what? When his watch has been broken, it is revealed that it was not an expensive one. What difference does that make to the question of culpability? Even more instructive is the way in which the demands of the plot undermine the character attributed to Mr Curry. He is represented as a misanthropist. Nevertheless, he has to be present at the party, and as the Browns would not invite such a person he has to appear as a gate-crasher, which is a strange role for a misanthropist. Moreover the plot requires that when Paddington requests the loan of a watch to conjure with it should be Mr Curry who offers his, which is hardly the act of an unsympathetic man.

The way in which these details are intended to manipulate the reader's sympathy can readily be perceived by readers of the age-group for which it caters. The reason why they are necessary, however, is beyond their ken. Despite a certain sophistication, *A Bear Called Paddington* is a book for the very young. It cannot therefore afford to attempt the dramatic division of the reader's sympathies between opposed characters which is the hallmark of a developed novel.

4

THE TOWER BY THE SEA

MEINDERT DEJONG'S *The Tower by the Sea* is a fable illustrating the proposition that 'All God's creatures have a right to live'. It evokes a world of moral certainty and of sure results: 'Because she was wise, she was also merciful.' In it ignorance leads inevitably, through fear, to superstition and frenzied cruelty. Above all it exalts the virtues of a quiet rationality—which is allied to feeling but not governed by it: 'Now let us be done with nonsense' says the wise old woman at the extremely moving climax. And she says it 'sharply'.

Put like this it may be felt that the child critic is being offered something very unattractive indeed—in spite of the delight which children find in making their own firm moral judgements. But we are not back to the crude lessons and pieties of Hannah More. For the complexity of *The Tower by the Sea*, like the complexity of George Eliot's novels for the adult, renders it the very opposite of a piece of repulsive moralising. The pill is sugar throughout while remaining a pill. And it is this, together with certain things that may be learned about the writer's use of language in fiction, which leads us to recommend the book, even above others by its distinguished author.

The complexity is not complication. The plot could be adequately given in a few breathless sentences. It is the result of the consummate handling of our sympathies. This starts immediately with the magpie, the first subject of the fable's great maxim 'All God's creatures have a right to live'.

She had found the fledgling magpie out of its nest on a cold, early day in spring when the hoar frost makes each blade of grass stand stiff and white like a frosted spear. There among the spears of grass lay the shivering magpie.

But a page and a half sufficed to turn the poor little creature in its wonderfully evoked stark environment into an animal version of the human type most detested by Conrad: 'Pesky and busy and wicked and noisy.' A *real* magpie in fact, inviting on the reader's part no particular sympathy, and certainly no sentimentality, however resolute. Yet 'The old woman loved it.' If we should now ask our pupils, 'Do you like that magpie?' they may begin to see the fuller force of the old woman's maxim.

Immediately a contrast is given in the stupid cruelty of the dune farmer (a person who might well be prey to a belief in maxims) to the white kitten. The stupidity is given as full a force as the cruelty: 'what made this evil seem still more evil to the farmer was that this witches' cat was white, instead of black as witches' cats should be'. Then he bungles the drowning, and begins to get out his absurd apparatus of brooms and crossings and mumblings. The wise old woman luckily saves the kitten. She does this from natural compassion, but also—we should note—on rational principle: 'Now you be still' she says to the jealous magpie. 'This kitten, too, wanted to live.'

The fable turns to wider issues. There is a description of the general state of superstition, and this is especially linked with the 'hag-ridden old crones'. Is this a curious, or even violent, attack on the sympathies of those children who admire their Nannas, or an unsought outlet for those who don't? It is neither if attention is directed by the teacher at this point to the confounding fact that the heroine of the tale is also an old woman: and if the question is asked, 'Have we yet encountered any other old woman?'—we have, because the whole tale is that which 'the old nursemaids and grandmothers of Katverloren to this day tell to the children of Katverloren'. The case is still undecided, both for magpies and old women.

In ten pages, then, we have ample material for eliciting complexity of response without mystification. To this we should add what shortly ensues: the triumph of rational compassion (or good government) in the wise old woman's training of the cat, who has changed from a pitiful and fascinating kitten into an equally fascinating leaping carnivore 'steely claws spread and wickedly reaching'. The wise old woman's maxim is further drained of sentimentality or careless ease of assent. The cat, who *is* now a cat, is curbed by pain. Later an older child may recognise the parallel between this and the cat's ability to rock the cradle and the Burgomaster's baby to safety. For present purposes, however, we have said enough to indicate the kind of response invited by the first few pages of the book. It is our opinion that this level is maintained, with only slight lapses, throughout.

In fact the fable becomes more complex. Teachers might, for example, find it useful to ask at appropriate points questions which imply much more than mere comprehension on the part of their eight- or twelve-year-olds. They might ask:

'Why is it that the cat walking down the village street with the magpie fluttering above "no higher than a man's head" is indeed a disquieting vision, even though we know why they do it?

'Why is it that the cat's balancing of the cot on the sea *is* a "miracle" and beautiful, even though we know how it came about?

'Why is it that the crones who become menacingly evil are so often presented as just rather silly—the "heroine" who beat off Satan with a broom being explicitly described as "The old liar! The dust from the turf bin was still on her black woollen apron."

'Why is it that we don't mind the villagers' surreptitious removal of the marks of their well deserved shame—the stake and the wood for burning?

'Why do we feel that the vilely cruel treatment of the cat by the boys and men seems natural and even healthy compared to crossed brooms and irrational fears (even though it appears, at the end, as one of the features of Katverloren life which is explicitly condemned)?

'What relation has Alice's touching superstitious terror on behalf of babies to the superstition of the villagers, and the rationality of the wise old woman?'

Many more such questions will naturally arise in the reading of so finely wrought a fable. But we would like to suggest, finally, that *The Tower by the Sea* also offers considerable opportunity, even to its youngest readers, to recognise the uses of language in fiction. The most obvious way to indicate this would be to ask pupils about the occurrence of the words 'know' and 'fact' in the book. This point is not over-subtle. They are almost always used, and insistently used, when describing the delusions of superstition: 'The old crones *knew* this' (author's italics) is merely typical. Children might be alerted early on in class reading to watch for this—and then asked why such plain words are used thus. The teacher will have a bigger word—Irony. As we have noted he *need* not use it, but he could easily point to its effects—its real effects as opposed to its blanketing air of authority. The sentences: 'Men, feeling good, stood in groups on street corners, hands deep in pockets. They laughed a lot, studied the sky, tossed remarks at young women hurrying by, tossed an idle stone at a dog or cat, studied the sky', might, for example, repay the class's attention. Why does the author make the men study the sky twice? What relation does this repetition have to the description of their other activities? Are they really laughing?

Is there any point in repeating 'tossed'? Isn't the author trying to get at you through placing his words in a certain pattern instead of getting on with the story? If so, how? And so on. The daring teacher might even try the effect of asking why 'God' should be omitted in the two mirror paragraphs at the beginning of page 34.

There are many other examples. We wish merely to suggest at present that *The Tower by the Sea* offers rich opportunities to the child critic: through a genuine complexity based on very reassuring grounds, and through a subtle and functional art.

5

DAWN WIND

It is notable, though not strange, that much writing for older children is set in the past. An obvious reason for this is that it allows—carrying on from *Little Black Sambo* and *Babar*—a full play of fantasy, a condition where, to use Henry James's terms about Romance, the balloon of experience with its car of imagination is cut free from ties with the earth. More responsibly, as in Meindert DeJong, it allows the author to develop the truth of his fable unimpeded by the known and possibly contradictory data of everyday life. It is a convention both romantic and satisfyingly malleable. And it does not *necessarily* involve any concern with the past as such. DeJong gives us a convincing account of superstition, but his *point of view* is modern.

In the best work of Rosemary Sutcliff, however, there is additional matter, and therefore a new kind of complexity. For she challenges us to take her history *seriously*, to get inside the minds of her remote heroes instead of merely borrowing the trappings of their world.* It is dimly like reading Homer to read her account, for example, of being inside a gladiator's helmet at the beginning of *The Mark of the Horse Lord*: we see through the eye slits and share the

---

* By 'history' in this context we mean, of course, an imaginative re-creation. Many of the periods with which Rosemary Sutcliff deals are extremely obscure. But this does not affect the present point.

protagonist's sense of blood, the arena, and aims which are not ethical or glamorous but bent on mere survival. Ethics and glamour come later, of course: but they are powerful by *analogy* with our assumptions rather than by *identity* with them.

We consider it axiomatic that a truly internal sense of the past, of an alien but substantial world, is of educative value to children (and others). And it is the creation of this which makes Rosemary Sutcliff a rare and distinguished writer.

But this is not a full account. Rosemary Sutcliff is also clearly—sometimes too clearly—a very deliberate artist. Her books are highly—sometimes too highly—shaped and worked together. They at once draw on and re-create a sense of the 'mythic': of purposive patterns to be seen in history and through the personal destinies of her characters. We will now suggest how, in reading one of her finest books, *Dawn Wind*, the child critic may be urged to feel and to reconcile these characteristics, and to experience something new.

First, and most simply, attention can be directed to the means by which authenticity is given to the remote life of sixth-century Britain. Not the least exciting of these are the numerous episodes where strangeness is very explicit. Against a background of abandoned Roman towns and shrines we are given in great detail the life and customs of Saxon warrior farmers: the thralls, the Bride-Race, Frey's horse, the throne of King Aethelbert standing in the marshes, and so on. These, however, could be mere trappings if they were not supported by the emotional participation invited in other episodes—Owain's swearing of the pagan war-oath at the horse sacrifice (Chapter XV) or his experience of the boar hunt (Chapter XIX). Such things are climaxes, and powerfully felt: but even *they* could be relatively external if it were not for the intimate texture of Rosemary Sutcliff's prose. And it is *here* that the pupil might usefully be given guidance. The teacher may feel, as do we, that some effects are a little too carefully and insistently poetic and 'concrete'

Dawn Wind

—the first page and a half of the book being an example. He may even like to ask a class which is already sympathetically on the side of the novel whether they think some things rather overdone: he could, for example, propose a comparison between the plain success of a metaphor like 'the weeks he had spent here in the shelter of Priscilla's kindness had had a kind of battered peace about them, like the lull in a storm' (page 22), and the insistence on Regina's eyes as a 'strange rain-grey' (pages 37, 39, 46 and elsewhere). But if this, as it may well be, is felt to be far too confusing (advanced?) for the pupil, it is certainly essential to point to other details which unobtrusively but consistently give the true *substance* to an alien past: 'getting unsteadily to his feet once more, he stood looking about him and sniffing, to get some idea of his direction' (page 8). That word 'sniffing' could well be discussed, as could Owain's later ability to smell the onset of a storm. The discussion would be about the *implications* of such animal awareness; it might eventually reach out to touch on its relation to the complicated questions of civilisation which are the main subject of the book. Similar effects abound: the reference of the prose is never to other than a sixth-century reality—distances are measured in bow-shots or spear-throws; Lords have a supra-personal authority which not only presides over the King's hunt but makes phrases like 'said the voice of Gerontius, Prince of Powys' an unaffected and acceptable substitute in modern English for 'said Gerontius'; and, even more artfully, casual illustrations are given from the sixth-century point of view but in the present tense, as though they belonged to our world, 'Haegel had come, unheralded and alone, *as a man may* drop in to sit by a friend's hearth and drink his ale and re-fight old battles or discuss the harvest prospects' (page 87, our italics). Such details, we suggest, create the historical sense. The discovery of their implications and their place in the novel is a critical enterprise rather than a comprehension exercise. And it follows that in being alerted to them the pupil is being enabled to see the book as a work of art. One is moved at a depth entirely appropriate to the subject and its ideal audience.

This, of course, leads directly to our second point about—for want of a more exact word—the 'form' of the book. It will be clear to the teacher who has read *Dawn Wind* through beforehand that its dominating concern, exemplified in Owain's adventures and in the development of his sensibility, is the gradual evolution from the 'darkness' of the destruction of the remnant of Romano-British Christian civilisation by the Saxons, to the birth (the dawn wind) of a new Anglo-Saxon civilisation and a new Christianity. (The teacher who is a Welsh nationalist may find further interests, and prefer Owen to Gawain.) But in class reading it will be necessary to trace the stages of the story, and to elicit their significance by questions aimed at the pupil's critical awareness of what is going forward at deeper levels. Such questions readily come to mind. Why, after the initial defeat and loss, does Owain feel obliged to leave behind the substitute parentage of Priscus and Priscilla, who are clear and admirable representatives of the dying civilisation? Of what importance is it that the brutal cattle raiders at Viroconium are British?* What is Rosemary Sutcliff suggesting in the scene of Dog's burial when Owain is distracted from suicide by the discovery of a Roman mosaic which evokes Regina and her symbolic properties of plants and birds? What stage is marked by the description of Owain's mood when he first becomes a Saxon warrior?:

> ... he alone had no roots in it. He had taken the war-oath with these men, he was bound to them and they to him, and yet he was cut off from them. He was British and they were Saxon, and between the two lay all the gulf that could lie between two worlds; but dimly he realised that there was another gulf between them also. They had some-

---

* A passage after the latter episode is clearly placed as a key one in respect to these questions.

Dawn Wind

thing to fight for; he had only something to fight against. It was a curiously desolate feeling.

And what is the relation of this to the mood just before the battle of Wodensbeorg?:

> ... the strange thing was that he never for one moment thought of going back to Priscus and Priscilla. If he had found the remnants of a British host and marched out with them again to face the Saxon hordes, he might have gone back one day, if he had lived; even, perhaps, if the men last night had been Saxon raiders. But Britain was a lost land and a lost cause, the swords were rusted and the lights were out, and nothing seemed left to do but to get away and leave it to the dark.
> Suddenly he knew that like the men on either side of him, he had something to fight for, and not, as he had once thought, only something to fight against. He was one of the men crouching in the woods beyond Wodensbeorg, waiting to go into battle for the sake of a frontier and a free people among the Western Hills. And in that instant with the knowledge of his oneness with them, he was one with the Saxon warriors at his shoulders. 'One band, one brotherhood. . . .'

What has caused the change, and *to* what is it leading Owain and the reader? What are we to make of Owain's reaction to the news of Ceawlin's death—that he and his two sons had made the 'best showing'? Why is Aethelbert, wily welcomer of the stern new Christianity, the only Saxon King to reside in the remnant of a Roman town? Why is the new Christianity made to seem so rigid, even arrogant, in comparison to that of the British village at the beginning of the book? Has Owain's final, rather muted, return to Regina any kind of relation to the larger political and religious movement of the novel? Why *is* it muted? By questions of this sort we may hope to awaken and confirm a sense of the formal unity, the controlled and significant flow of the work. And this will naturally be seen not as an abstract model, but as a thing very much one with, and dependent on, the remarkable historical authenticity.

Realising the rich pattern thus produced should, we feel, be sufficient critical exercise for the child reader. The suggestion of less satisfactory elements in *Dawn Wind* will rightly hold second place, unless these actually hinder the process of reading. If it *were* felt that the play of coincidence —Owain's saving of Beornwulf, the appearances of Einon Hên, and so on—is a little too neat, too literally providential, then free discussion would certainly be in place— most fruitfully in terms of 'convention', i.e. the kind of story this is. And we have already glanced at possible difficulties arising from an occasionally over-rich style. But these features will not, we think, be found to play a very large or unacceptable role. The pupil is unlikely to feel much of the justifiable disappointment which is at the root of adverse criticism. In this case the discrimination best encouraged in teaching will take the form of ignoring, or passing by. If, however, some jolt to raptness is, in practice, felt to be desirable, then we would recommend a consideration of Vadir: his tendency to resemble (leaving Lord Byron out of it) the bad hero in a Western: the failure to present sufficiently his paradoxical attractiveness for Owain: and his rather too prepared and neat death.

But the teacher's main concern here is nevertheless the elicitation of a full response to an achievement which is much more complex than any have so far considered, and which derives its great force from the creation of a culture profoundly different from our own within a structure which compels enhanced attention to the meaning of the whole.

6

TREASURE ISLAND

THE opening words of *Treasure Island* lines up one side—'Squire Trelawney, Dr Livesey, and the rest of these gentlemen . . .'—in terms which make it clear enough that Jim is not a full member. In the mouth of a speaker who was a 'gentleman' that classifying use of the word would have been ironical or patronising. Of course, in a room full of children who want to get on with the story, this kind of analysis is out of place. All the same, it is necessary to establish as quickly as possible that their wholehearted sympathy is not being solicited for Squire Trelawney and his lieutenants. Even before the opening sentence has ended we have been introduced to 'the brown old seaman with the sabre cut', fit object for a romantic interest which it would be fatal to deny, and yet which cannot be admitted without taking a limiting view of Squire Trelawney and his friends, who do not share it.

Many children who read *Treasure Island* at school find it boring, and, treated as a plain tale of good 'uns versus bad 'uns, so it is. To treat it in that manner, however, is to do a vitally complex novel an injustice. Although it is not plain, all that is required for its richness to be appreciated is for the reader to give his natural sympathies full play. But as our natural sympathies are contradictory, this process is by no means simple in its consequences. There is no character, not even Jim Hawkins himself, who does not at times alienate us. When it comes to taking sides, none of the three groups of characters—the authorities, the law-abiding, and the delinquent—satisfies.

Patronised from the first chapter onwards by the authorities (like Dr Livesey), and similarly terrorised by the delinquents (like Billy Bones), the law-abiding are the feeblest and least interesting group; yet it would be hypocritical to deny that we sympathise with them. They are the most like us. We too, like Jim's father, would have shrunk from demanding payment from a homicidal desperado, and yet, like the locals at the *Admiral Benbow*, would have relished his stories 'about hanging, and walking the plank, and storms at sea, and the Dry Tortugas, and wild deeds and places on the Spanish Main'. There are many questions to be asked about the law-abiding, which start 'Can you honestly blame . . .?' Can you, for example, honestly blame the villagers for refusing to give positive help to Jim and his mother, when they realised that pirates were going to raid the inn? Or can you blame the widow herself for her blind persistence in recovering her legal dues? Can you blame Tom, the honest sailor, for being so fatally helpless in his dealings with Silver (in Chapter XIV)? There is point in remembering, when reading a story of this kind, that we ourselves are to some degree puny. Nor need we be completely humble about it. Our comparative feebleness enables us, however dishonestly, to retain certain human feelings which the authorities and the delinquent alike have either outgrown or simply lost.

After the murder of Tom the honest sailor, and the obsequious demise of Tom Redruth the gamekeeper in Chapter XVIII, the only representative of the law-abiding in the tale is Jim Hawkins himself. Our interest in him, of course, goes far beyond a recognition of this fact. He stands out from the rest of the law-abiding as distinctly as Silver stands out from the rest of the delinquent characters. They are both special cases, as Captain Smollett realises as soon as he claps eyes on them. ('I'll have no favourites on my ship' —Chapter IX.) Nevertheless, it is important to realise that he *is* a law-abiding character, and his retention of human feelings is purchased at the cost of a certain self-deception on his part (and perhaps that of Stevenson). Note the innocuous way in which he saves his life (in Chapter XXVI) by shooting Israel Hands—'I am sure it was without conscious aim'—or the ambiguity of his justification for leaving the surviving pirates marooned on the island—'It went to all our hearts, I think, to leave them in that wretched state; but we could not risk another mutiny; and to take them home for the gibbet would have been a cruel sort of kindness' (Chapter XXXIV).

This blindness does not act only to shield Jim himself by requiring the reader to supplement Jim's vision with his own. It also serves to shield the authorities. Like Ben Gunn, Jim has complete confidence in 'a gen'leman born'. He is no more capable of criticising one than is Tom Redruth, who, when the Squire asks him to forgive him for bringing him to his death, asks: 'Would that be respectful like, from me to you?' He never questions their right to take over the treasure map. Although he faithfully records Dr Livesey's comments on the Squire's indiscretion (in Chapter VI), he adds no comments of his own. Although his portrayal of Captain Smollett betrays no personal enthusiasm, this lack of warmth is not a sign of disapproval: it is a sign of his respect for a perfect officer, of whom no less an authority than Dr Livesey remarks: 'That man Smollett is a better man than I am. And when I say that it means a deal, Jim' (Chapter XIX). As for Dr Livesey, Jim finds him always kind. Even when the doctor's decision to abandon the stockade has landed him in the arms of the pirates, he makes no reply to the explanation offered: 'I did what I thought best for those who had stood by their duty; and if you were not one of those, whose fault was it?' (Chapter XXXIII). Only at one point do we detect a flicker of something different. It comes in Chapter XV, when Ben Gunn is bargaining for a thousand pounds.

> '*And* a passage home?' he added, with a look of great shrewdness. 'Why,' I cried, 'the squire's a gentleman. And besides, if we got rid of the others, we should want you to help work the vessel home.'

It is Silver, not Jim, who remarks: 'I would set no limit to what gentlemen might consider shipshape'. (This is his reply to Captain Smollett's declaration, in Chapter XX, that rather than receive intelligence from a deserter, 'I would see you and him and this whole island blown clean out of the water into blazes first.') Jim's only criticism is expressed not in a word but in a deed: his refusal, in Chapter XXX, to break parole at Dr Livesey's instigation.

To get a clear view of the authorities it is necessary to ask the class what they would have said about Squire Trelawney and his friends, at this and that juncture, if they had been in Jim's shoes. There is, however, a danger here. In developing the pupil's awareness of this irony, the teacher encounters a problem similar to that encountered in a serious study of Shakespeare's *Henry V*. Once they realise that criticism of Squire Trelawney, Captain Smollett and Dr Livesey is admissible they can supply it endlessly, but to do so would be to depart too far from a true account of their reaction to the tale. The authorities may be complacent, callous and inflexible, but even so they are preferable to the delinquents. Order is preferable to disorder. To return to Chapter I, it comes undeniably as a relief when Dr Livesey quells Billy Bones in the Inn parlour. The way in which he exploits both his medical and his judicial authority to achieve this is, nevertheless, still questionable. ('If you keep on drinking rum . . . etc. If I catch a breath of complaint against you . . . etc.')

At this stage in the story, Dr Livesey has only demonstrated his possession of authority. In a public place it is not very difficult for a magistrate to turn his back on a threatening thug. When Tom, the loyal sailor, tries the same trick on a desert island (in Chapter XIV), the outcome is less heartening. Before the novel is over, however, the Doctor and 'the rest of these gentlemen' have demonstrated their title to the authority they possess by defeating a superior number of delinquents, in a fight with no holds barred. There is no cheating on Stevenson's part. He does not invent the handicaps which operate in the contest. Each advantage which the authorities enjoy in the struggle truly belongs to them. There may still be boy readers who regret that they win the final battle from ambush, instead of shooting it out in a straight fight where, now that the odds have been so drastically reduced in their favour, they stand a fair chance. But the intelligent anticipation shown on this occasion by the authorities, and the blinkered monomania of the delinquent, are qualities which have come by this time to be seen as characteristic. Anything different would be implausible.

It is in this context that the virtues of Captain Smollett and Dr Livesey must be insisted upon. Of course, these two professionals take command of the authorities as soon as the adventure gets under way. Self-indulgent Squire Trelawney fades into the background, his only useful quality being the marksmanship he exhibits in Chapter XVII. His authority vanishes the moment Captain Smollett asserts his rights as Master of the *Hispaniola*, establishing discipline and safeguarding the arms and ammunition. The captain's *forte* is inflexible adherence to regulations, demonstrated no less by the sentry roster in the stockade than in his refusal, when they parley, to grant Silver anything more than the promise of a fair trial. Respect for law, in fact, is shown to be a formidable advantage. The pirates' total lack of it reduces them to the level of a mob. The only basis for authority which they can recognise is fear. Thus neither Pew nor Silver can exercise command in moments of acute crisis. They do not even recognise that they will 'have to do sentry go, and ease off a point or so on the rum', until Ben Gunn has raided their camp and murdered one of them.

Captain Smollett's limited but admirable qualities are what the authorities need if they are to hold out against the delinquents. Additional and more repulsive qualities are needed in order to take the initiative and defeat them. These are possessed by hygienic Dr Livesey, who assumes effective command when the Captain has been wounded. Whereas the pirates are terrified of black spots, torn Bibles and ghostly voices, he is cool and rational. If the pirates are callous, so, but quite surgically, is he. Indeed, although a medical man, he regards ill health as an ally, and events bear out the view that 'It is something to have been an old soldier, but more still to have been a doctor.' It is not just that Billy Bones, Blind Pew, and Long John Silver are physically handicapped. The pirates further incapacitate themselves with rum, and neglect to take precautions against fever. The doctor assists in the latter effect. Recognising that the stockade is unhealthy he arranges for the pirates to camp there, while removing his own party to Ben Gunn's salubrious cave.

His greatest asset, however, is his alacrity. From the move from ship to stockade to the final successful ambush, the tactics of the authorities are decided by him. This quality of 'briskness', as Jim terms it, is the least agreeable feature of his entirely respectable but unsympathetic character, because it is part and parcel of a lack of feeling. Like some well-trained gymnast, he is always on his toes but never vital. He prescribes for the perils in which his party are involved without the least sign of being affected by them, remaining entirely business-like even at the moment of triumph.

Lack of feeling, however, is not only an intrinsic part of Dr Livesey's coolness. It is also an essential component of Captain Smollett's devotion to duty and of the ease with which Squire Trelawney takes everything for granted. The reader is continuously aware of this unresponsiveness, because it manifests itself in the mechanical quality of their relationship with Jim. 'This lad Hawkins is a trump, I perceive', is the initial acknowledgement he receives (in Chapter VI). When he discovers that Silver is planning to murder them—'they made me sit down at table beside them, poured me out a glass of wine, filled my hands with raisins, and all three, one after the other, and each with a bow, drank my good health' (Chapter XII). When Jim returns after his final critical adventure, the Squire 'was cordial and kind, saying nothing of my escapade, either in the way of blame or praise', while Captain Smollett goes out of his way to tell him that he will not sail with him again as he is 'too much of the born favourite'. No wonder Jim keeps sloping off. They take no personal note of him, so he might as well not be there. At the beginning of the book, on the other hand, Jim is somebody who really matters to Billy Bones. Billy knows he needs the boy. The need, moreover, is not merely practical.

To some extent, of course, this difference is a question of class, a subject on which the entire novel provides considerable food for thought. 'The men are not shy with him', Dr Livesey observes of Jim. The central point about Jim, however, is not that he is a commoner. So were his father and mother, but they did not enjoy his relationship with Billy Bones—'I was far less afraid of the captain himself than anybody else who knew him'. The central point about Jim is simply that he is a boy. This does not mean, of course, that he finds the pirates as a whole better company than the others. The pirates have no more time to play with him than have Squire Trelawney and his business-like friends. The pirates may not be business-like, but this does not make them free and easy. On the contrary, they are squalid, lazy, and dull, always murderously scampering after wealth, getting drunk, or performing cumbersome ceremonies. Billy Bones had collected sea-shells, but apart from Silver with his parrot none of the other pirates finds anything in life of interest except treasure, rum and rules. It is even difficult to imagine that they once amused themselves by making prisoners walk the plank.

It is here that Silver's distinction lies—not that he is the most sympathetic of all the characters in the book, but that he is pre-eminently entertaining. Above everything else—his coolness and courage, his intelligence and resilience, even his wife—he is most distinguished by his good cheer, a characteristic which is not diminished by the effort which at times we see it costs him. There is, for example, his ruminative speech, not just picturesquely nautical like that of the other pirates, but leisurely, reflective, even at time sententious—his 'King George's English' which at times he doubts his followers' capacity to understand. Although at times he betrays a rapacity no less obsessive than that of Israel Hands, he is capable of detached amusement at the successive problems which confront him. But his *joi-de-vivre* shows itself most of all in his playful hypocrisy, as when he touches his forelock 'with a solemn way he had' on mentioning a chaplain (Chapter X), or calls for an extra cheer for Captain Smollett when the latter calls for three cheers for the Squire (Chapter XII), or, at the very end, impertinently informs Captain Smollett that he has 'come back to my dooty, sir'. Comparison with the Uriah Heep style of Pew's false humility—'Will you give me your hand, my kind young friend, and lead me in?—reveals the special quality of Silver's Richard III-style irony. He plays with his victim's highest expectations. (Witness Squire Trelawney's enthusiastic letter, in Chapter VII.)

'Playing with' somebody, when that somebody is a child, can be either a highly appropriate activity or else a sinister one. This ambiguity dogs Silver's relationship with Jim from start to finish, investing it with a suspense of quite a different order from the what-will-happen-next suspense of the adventures. The question which expresses this deeper suspense poses itself continuously and is never answered: 'When all's said and done, is Silver Jim's friend?' From the first encounter with Jim at the sign of the 'Spy-Glass'

(Chapter VIII), the reader, unlike Jim, can see Silver's game, in the sense of his trickery, but he can also see that it is a game in the more innocent sense because the villain is so wholeheartedly enjoying it. And although he is clearly out to please the boy in order to deceive him, the fact remains that he succeeds so well, much better indeed than the virtuous characters, who do not even try. He shows an understanding which can only come from sympathy, however ironic. Although Jim has been tricked, therefore, the possibility that he has actually found a friend still remains, and whether the reader feels that he has indeed done so calls for a very sensitive reading of a passage like the following:

'Why, what a precious old sea-calf I am!' he said at last, wiping his cheeks. 'You and me should get on well, Hawkins, for I'll take my davy I should be rated ship's boy. But come now, stand by to go about. This won't do. Dooty is dooty, messmates. I'll put on my old cocked hat, and step along of you to Cap'n Trelawney and report this here affair. For, mind you, it's serious, young Hawkins; and neither you nor me's come out of it with what I should make so bold as to call credit. Nor you neither, says you; not smart—none of the pair of us smart. But dash my buttons! that was a good 'un about my score.'

And he began to laugh again, and that so heartily, that though I did not see the joke as he did, I was again obliged to join in his mirth.

On our little walk along the quays, he made himself the most interesting companion, telling me about the different ships that we passed by, their rig, tonnage, and nationality, explaining the work that was going forward—how one was discharging, another taking in cargo, and a third making ready for sea; and every now and then telling me some little anecdote of ships or seamen, or repeating a nautical phrase till I had learned it perfectly. I began to see that here was one of the best of possible shipmates.

The problem is not 'what does that add up to?', but the more interesting 'what do I make of that?', wedding reader and text.

As the plot develops, uncertainty about Silver's attitude to Jim adds an extra dimension to the interest of the incidents. What would have happened in Chapter XI, for example, if Jim had been discovered hiding in the apple barrel? Or if Silver had spotted him watching from the undergrowth, when he murdered Tom the loyal sailor, in Chapter XIV? The reader fears he knows the answer, but he would almost like it to happen, in order to make sure, and possibly be proved wrong.

Despite the first-person narrative, a similar uncertainty attaches to Jim's own feelings about Silver, once he knows the truth about him. He dutifully applies opprobrious epithets—'the monster had pulled himself together, his crutch under his arm' (Chapter XIV). He also fair-mindedly expresses admiration for Silver's heroic qualities—'he was brave and no mistake' (Chapter XXVIII). But there is something more. Thus, when he is in the apple barrel he hears Silver flatter the sailor he is suborning by calling him 'as smart as paint'.

> You may imagine how I felt when I heard this abominable old rogue addressing another in the very same terms of flattery as he had used to myself. I think, if I had been able, that I would have killed him through the barrel.

After witnessing Tom's murder, he has no more illusions about Silver's good nature, but the reader's sense of a special relationship remains. When, at the end of Silver's embassy to the besieged party in the stockade, Captain Smollett leaves the cripple to fend for himself, why do we feel that the boy checks an impulse to help him to his feet? He does not admit to this weakness, which doubtless he would think proper to suppress, it being tantamount to criticism of his commanding officer. 'Not a man among us moved', is all he tells us, but the suggestion that this is a startling fact speaks volumes because of our sense of a special tie between them.

This sense of a special tie is amply and yet subtly justified when Jim becomes the pirates' prisoner. Tactical considerations eventually make it advisable for Silver to protect the boy, while it is his word of honour, not his personal inclination, which compels the boy to stay at Silver's side. This tactical and legal account, however, ignores the personal factors which also operate, and whose presence is felt in the narrative. The reader's pleasure in their re-union is shared by one at least of the two characters. At least his initial invitation to Jim to join the gang must be taken at its face value: he stands to gain nothing by it.

> 'Now, you see, Jim, so be as you *are* here,' says he, 'I'll give you a piece of my mind. I've always liked you, I have, for a lad of spirit, and the picter of my own self when I was young and handsome. I always wanted you to jine and take your share, and die a gentleman, and now, my cock, you've got to.'

A few minutes later, however, although he is risking his life to save Jim's, his motives are ambiguous again. Pure policy cannot explain the gloriously avuncular touch of handing the boy the black spot to keep as a curiosity, at the end of Chapter XXIX. Pure friendship cannot be reconciled with the murderous glances he darts at Jim as he hauls him up the hill, in Chapter XXXII.

Jim's own feelings remain similarly ambiguous. Witness his words when he has rejected Silver's offer of membership of the gang: 'And now, Mr Silver,' I said, 'I believe you're the best man here, and if things go the worst, I'll take it kind of you to let the doctor know the way I took it.' The Doctor himself could not have spoken more superciliously. But it is Jim, not the Doctor, speaking: consequently, behind his words lies an implicit reproach, and perhaps even a not quite desperate appeal. Nor would the Doctor have watched so closely to determine the effect of his words.

> 'I'll bear it in mind,' said Silver, with an accent so curious that I could not, for the life of me, decide whether he were laughing at my request, or had been favourably affected by my courage.

It is easy to exaggerate this point. The moment is critical. Jim has sufficient practical reasons to be anxious about Silver's feelings, without personal ones being needed to explain his interest in them. There is, however, no practical reason for his continuing with this preoccupation even after Silver is finally committed to his side.

> He looked at me and nodded, as much as to say, 'Here is a narrow corner', as indeed I thought it was. His looks were now quite friendly; and I was so revolted at these constant changes, that I could not forbear whispering, 'So you've changed sides again.'

They may not be friends, but they matter to each other in a way which no other characters in this novel do. The fact that their relationship cannot be classified is far from meaning that it is not, as presented, a real one. Indeed, they matter to each other in a way rare in children's fiction, a way which offers insights of the kind which only fiction can offer.

7

HUCKLEBERRY FINN

DOUGLAS BROWN in *Young Writers, Young Readers* warns the teacher against treating *Treasure Island* as a simple adventure story. Perhaps the same danger does not threaten a reading of *Huckleberry Finn*. Its classical status is internationally recognised—it is a great children's story, and very much more. Nevertheless, there is a danger that the book's importance will be equated, by a modern class, with its treatment of 'the Negro problem'. This problem is certainly central to the action, but only as a focus of a more universal problem. It is the teacher's task to bring this focus to bear.

The true critical reference is, we suggest, not to Bret Harte, or even Harriet Beecher Stowe, but to a tradition of Anglo-Saxon writing, of which Ben Jonson and Swift are the most notable representatives. The tradition is one of creative *disgust*. *Huckleberry Finn* is a book about cant.

Cant is, of course, rightly associated with hypocrisy. It manifests itself, however, and most exuberantly in this book, as a feature of *language*. Consider, for example, Huck's father's denunciation of the iniquities of 'govment' (Chapter VI); the special and charming professional skills of the King and the Duke (passim); and Tom Sawyer's romantic vocabulary. Contrast with these the natural speech of Jim, and the way in which, despite his humble acceptance—and even admiration of—more grandiose registers, Huck sticks to his own plain idiom. This idiom is a vehicle for complex ironies which depend upon the easily felt comparison with other, artificial, forms of speech—a fact which is lost sight of by critics who hail it as, in itself, achieving an American (non-correct) *classical* quality.

As Twain himself remarked in his introductory note, a reader who got the impression of different characters 'trying to talk alike and not succeeding' would be imperceptive.

The teacher will, however, naturally draw the class's attention to various forms of speech only as an indication of what the characters are up to. After all, Swift's objection to cant was not simply one of linguistic purism. It was that departures from linguistic norms are signs of departures from moral norms. For him the norm of behaviour and speech was that of the 'man of good sense'—the civilised gentleman. What is distinctively American about Twain is that his norm is that of the child of nature—whose major dread is of being civilised. *Both* these norms, however, are directly opposed to the cruelty and false pride of human nature, which find their most vicious form in the mob *and* in those who, while exploiting the mob, pander to it. Cant is at once the instrument and the expression of depravity. Such considerations are important, and need to be elicited from and enforced by the child critic, because otherwise large stretches of the novel will be found disappointing. The story of the family feud, for example—the destruction of the sympathetic Col Grangerford and his sons—lacks the colourfulness and excitement which it seems to promise. Instead of high adventure we are presented with grey, mechanical, and unrevenged death. Huck does well to get out. The teacher should ask the class why—and why Jim's welcome 'is that you, honey?' does not sound mawkish. Answers are likely to be complicated.

What is attractive about Col Grangerford, beside his gentlemanly courtesy and domestic power, is that he is both brave and individual. He challenges comparison with Col Sherburn—another calm and strong man, an exception to

Huckleberry Finn

his own rule that 'the average man's a coward'. The extraordinary and ambiguous scenes (Chapters XXI and XXII) in which Sherburn commits cold-blooded murder and then repulses the lynch mob by sheer 'character' *almost* convinces us that it does not matter what happens to average men. Characteristically Huck, here perhaps our moral mentor, can only resolve the situation by escape—escape from the code of gentlemanly toughness as well as that of the canaille. He had not shared the feeling of the contemptible mob: *he* did not have to slink away. However: 'I could a staid, if I'd wanted to, but I didn't want to.' Much of the action of the novel—in a way its central concern—is the escape from people and their codes: from the Widow Douglas, from Huck's father, and (most difficult of all) from the King and the Duke. When we last hear from him, Huck is planning to 'light out for the territory ahead of the rest'. Home is a floating house on a river which skirts, but is not contaminated by, the abodes of men.

If this were a complete account the great American Humorist would already be, in *Huckleberry Finn*, the total misanthropist which he later became. However, even in the drab incidents mentioned there are touches of a pathos inconsistent with the Swiftian view. The book is, after all, as cheerful as it is nasty.

There are people who have direct feelings—the lovers separated by the feud, and Boggs' bereaved daughter. There are also many such details as young Sheperdson's refusal, whatever the reason, to fire when he has Buck in his sights (the class might look out for some of them). Human nature is not entirely unredeemable.

This human quality is of course most manifest in Huck—manifest in his inability to refuse help. 'Miss Mary Jane, you can't abear to see people in trouble, and *I* can't—most always.' (Chapter XXVIII). Thus it comes about that the central concern of Huck, and therefore of the novel, is no less rescuing people than escaping from them. He is not just errant, but also a knight errant. This humane role, however, does not involve a humanistic optimism. Indeed, it is selective, not because it is critical but because it is impulsive. Huck and Jim feel and register all the evidence for adverse judgement, but ostentatiously leave the reader to judge. Even the King's stink is at first explained as being probably a natural feature of royalty, unpleasant but not to be held against him. In the same way, the attempt to defraud Mary Jane and her sisters is something to be thwarted, but not something which deserves tarring and feathering and being run out of town on a rail. We are all struck by Huck's imperturbable desire to warn the King and the Duke *after* they have betrayed Jim for a sordid $40. The odd thing is that this complete disregard of 'ornery' social values should go with an obstinate decency. Why is such decency felt as credible? Because, surely, Huck's factual approach is the most natural thing in the world ('child of nature'): and the second most natural thing is *sympathy*.

Both qualities are linked in the novel by their power to resist cant. Huck is in possession of many useful facts—for example he knows that a man's corpse floats face down (Chapter III). It might then appear that Tom's story of an oriental caravan on the banks of the Mississippi would not take him in. He believes it, however, because the only use *he* has for language is to convey fact or to conceal it. He has no use for fantasy, although he finds many uses for lies. Thus when in Chapter III Miss Watson tells him of the efficacy of prayer he tries it out and finds it, in his own way, singularly wanting, just as, after the misfortune of Chapter X, he accepts the 'nigger' lore concerning the malevolent effects of snake-skins. This kind of test, however, *cannot* be applied to codes of behaviour in which obedience is its own reward—i.e. which cannot be directly proved or disproved from experience. For example, Huck has been told that it is wrong to steal. His sense of fact has little bearing on this commandment, either in the case of Watermelons or in that of Jim. Theoretically it can be valid whatever the facts: in practice, however, Huck's sympathy—the natural associate of his literalness—can prevent obedience, even when the facts do not.

Twain has thus created a character whose implicit moral alignment has the same satirical bearing as the explicit doctrinal allegiance of Candide. But whereas Candide is subject merely to doubts, Huck is subject to painful moral conflicts (and is therefore the hero of a novel, not a fable). These conflicts are, of course, the result of a clash between what Twain makes us feel to be *innate* goodness and a 'virtue' which lends itself to cant. The central and poignant irony of the book is that *Huck* does not realise this. His choice of virtue is, for him, a determination to go to Hell. The path of goodness is the broad and easy one. This point might appear to be complex, but in fact Twain drives it home with a sledge-hammer in Chapter XXXI.

Before proceeding to apply these observations in the analysis of a particular passage, certain concomitants should be pointed out. Natural sympathy is limited in range: it cannot be felt 'on principle'. It is not felt for classes of people, but only for individuals. Thus while Huck is *not* an Abolitionist he wants to help, not only his friend Jim, but also the slave family which is broken up when the King sells them down the river. Thus he feels sympathy for Mary Jane and her sisters but not for the revivalist congregation which the King earlier fools. Similarly, he has no sympathy for thugs *in general*, but tries to save the three on the stranded paddle-steamer. It is, in short, the helpless who are exempted from Twain's misanthropy. The most salient and moving presentation of this impulse comes at the end of Chapter XXIII, in Jim's story about his deaf child. But as regards able-bodied humanity in the mass, Twain's attitude is that they get what they deserve—with no help from Huck. There is even an element of *schadenfreude* in watching them get it.

All these points cannot, of course, be established immediately. As one incident succeeds another, different aspects of the complex attitude implicit in the novel emerge, and should be elicited. For a start, the teacher might ask how it is that in Chapter I Twain's irony is directed at everyone *except* Huck, despite the latter's apparent naivety. When he describes the widow's saying grace as the way in which she would 'grumble a little over the victuals', why is it that we do not just dismiss this as evidence of his ignorance?—possibly because it *is* civilised. By continuously taking such bearings from the pupils' own sympathies—and prejudices—as the story unfolds, the class should, however, be able to recognise what is so fully characteristic of Chapter XVI by the time they come to it. What is needed above all is that they should be qualified to complement Huck's judgements with their own, and yet that their own additional judgements should have been formed from responses to what they have already read.

Chapter XVI is the finest example of the delicate yet decisive art with which Twain uses Huck's voice to convey *ab extra* the recurrent climaxes of his moral education. This is a case—*the* case—where Huck instinctively chooses the good as opposed to the conventionally virtuous. To distinguish their own consciousness of the situation from Huck's, the class should be invited to compare their reaction to Jim's plan for the future with Huck's: 'He was saying how the first thing he would do when he got to a free State he would go to saving up money and never spend a single cent, and when he got enough he would buy his wife. . . . It most froze me to hear such talk. He wouldn't ever dared to talk such talk in his life before.' This would prepare the class for the *force* of Huck's 'conscience' in a society which did (does?) not consider as an axiom that everyone is 'white inside'—or even human. It is a force demonstrated by a marvellously created social context which reaches as low in the social scale as Huck himself, and is expressed by the proverbial wisdom of 'give a nigger an inch and he'll take an ell'. Now, *we*—and most of Twain's original post-Civil-War readers—*know* what wicked nonsense all this is. But does Huck? After all it is true that he is helping Jim to steal himself—a whole $800 worth: 'Conscience says to me, "What had poor Miss Watson done to you, that you could see her nigger go off right under your eyes and never say one single word? What did that poor old woman do to you, that you could treat her so mean? Why, she tried to learn you your book, she tried to learn you your manners, she tried to be good to you every way she knowed how. *That's* what she done." ' In the action which follows Huck is in fact denying the civilisation which is so subtly obtruded in the penultimate sentence. So it is a real conflict, only temporarily quieted by his 'virtuous' resolve to give Jim up.

But then he meets the two nigger-hunters, and strange things begin to happen. First, Huck's innate goodness sweeps everything forward in a series of superbly calculated lies. The situation thus becomes a catalyst for actions which transcend the purely black-white problem. The men on the boat are, in a very limited sense, decent—even civilised. Their speech suggests that they are gentlemen born, and they are very generous with conscience money. But the true crux is that they avoid—as we all tend to avoid—a dangerous call of Duty by a well-timed donation. They pay off the (supposed) sick *white* family—handsomely. And the class is left with the obvious, but subtle, reflection that these men have served to show the connection between 'virtue' and cash.

Huck's torment is caused by his seeing Jim (momentarily) as $800; and now *he* (and his supposed family) is paid for. And the reader needs this dramatic equation for any fair, as opposed to automatic, response to the problem of slavery. We are tactfully shown—that whatever else may be said— this institution breeds habits of mind which reduce all people to money. Huck sums up the particular case in a devastating manner. 'They went off, and I got aboard the raft feeling bad and low, because I knowed very well I had done wrong, and I see it warn't no use for me to try to learn to do right; a body that don't get *started* right when he's little, ain't got no show—when the pinch comes there ain't nothing to back him up and keep him to his work, and so he gets beat. Then I thought a minute, and says to myself, hold on—s'pose you'd a done right and give Jim up; would you felt better than what you do now? No, says I, I'd feel bad—I'd feel just the same way I do now. Well, then, says I, what's the use you learning to do right, when it's troublesome to do right and ain't no trouble to do wrong, and the wages is just the same? I was stuck.'

But the case is not only particular. We feel that this is but one illustration of F. R. Leavis's piercing remark that 'the essential theme of the book . . . is the complexity of ethical valuation in any society that has a complex tradition'. It is the teacher's task to bring out these implications.

This task is, however, by no means simple when we come to the final episodes of the book. There are aspects of these which invite a comparable ironic sympathy. For example, the way in which, while they (inefficiently) chain the runaway Jim, the Phelps also minister to his physical and spiritual needs. Similarly we are struck, as we have formerly been struck by the men in the boat, by the curious blend of prejudice and humanity in the plea of the old Doctor (Chapter XLII): 'Don't be no rougher on him than your're obleeged to, because he aint a bad nigger. . . .'. In fact, perhaps, this speech sums up more succinctly than anything else in the book, both the values and the limitations of the civilisation from whose margin Huck addresses us.

The narrative of the last chapters, however, centres, of course, on the antics of Tom Sawyer. These could not be treated in the same way. The American Humorist takes over while Huck fades out. It is supposed to be Huck speaking: but what he has to say omits all those considerations, prompted by irrepressible sympathy and good sense, which mark his account of Jim's previous tribulations. If Huck had continued to be *as* sympathetic, he would have refused to countenance Tom's antics, and the whole incident would have been eliminated. The class's attention can easily be drawn to this essential critical point by the question: 'Does

Huck continue to be Tom's friend?' If the answer is a qualified 'yes' then it should be further asked: 'What relation has this to his earlier sense of Jim's humanity irrespective of codes?' The hero is now Tom Sawyer, which means that a wilful denial of reality becomes a subject of approval because it is whimsical. Twain seems to be behind this. The Tom episodes *could* (by the determined critic) be seen as a kind of comic parallel and coda to the central conflict of the novel: that between codes and natural feeling. But the handling stresses only the laughable absurdity, not the serious implication.

How is this to be elicited in class? We have suggested that a responsive reading of the major part of the book cannot be continued to its close without a sense of disappointment. The question then is, quite simply, 'Is this disappointment shared by the class?' If it is, well and good; if it is not the teacher cannot inform his pupils that they are wrong. He may reflect that he has brought them to the book too early—but at least he will not get from children the kind of lofty nonsense offered by a Mr Sidnell (*The Cambridge Quarterly*, Vol. 2 No. 3, Summer 1967) who warns us in his flexible way that if we find these chapters amusing then, for us, 'there is no help . . . [We] would probably take Swift's *A Modest Proposal* at its face-value.'

8

GREAT EXPECTATIONS

DICKENS, the family favourite, is a different author to teach. And, curiously, this seems to be for reasons exactly the reverse of which led Dr Leavis to the famous judgement that he is mainly and merely a 'great entertainer'.* Whereas for the mature critic of twenty years ago Dickens's fantastic humours seemed fatally to deny him the status of a great artist, the immature critic of today appears reluctant to admit much humour at all. This may be a matter of social climate—with the traditional laughter and tears forced into shamed privacy—but it nevertheless leaves the teacher with a problem.

It is futile to explain a joke. Trabb's Boy and Mr Wopsle's *Hamlet* are either funny or they are not. It seems that for many pupils nowadays they are not. The problem is thus not one of resisting a fatal charm, but of establishing that there is charm at all.

We hope that these statements will prove to be extreme. But even if they are, the teacher will no doubt see the point of selecting *Great Expectations* for consideration. It is notoriously the least 'humorous' of Dickens's novels. Like *The Tempest* in Shakespeare's works, it has a relatively con-

---

* *The Great Tradition*, 1948. This judgement has since been very much modified.

ventional nature while not sacrificing very much the characteristic powers of the author. Unlike, for example, *Hard Times*, it is fully Dickensian: yet it is easy to approach from other ground.

If the Dickens charm is *not* felt, then approach assumes, of course, an unnatural importance. Author and Novel must be justified in the eyes of a newly literate solemnity. However, since most critics take the famous humour for granted, we feel that it first might be examined. The point of Trabb's Boy is obvious. We leave Wopsle's *Hamlet* to critical ingenuity (Pip's situation mirrored, or some such horror); but, more pertinently, the most prominent 'comic creation' in this novel rewards closer scrutiny. Pumblechook, although a magnificent individual, is typical of Dickens. (Which is why he is so individual.) He is a comic villain in the line of Uriah Heep, Pecksniff, Chadband and many others. And the main point about him is that he is not, ultimately, *comical* at all. Whether or not his 'May I . . . ?', etc., is found *funny*, a class might be asked what they make of his final interview with Pip at the *Blue Boar*. Here he is the same as always. His speech is still absurdly orotund. His pretensions are as preposterous and as successful as ever. He reveals no sudden villainous streak. Yet, Pip's childhood and his prosperous phase having passed, Pumblechook's behaviour is felt as really repulsive. He, unchanged, is now intolerable for Pip, and for us. And the changed *response* is significant for any view of Dickens's comedy. A character who is at first merely entertaining—a 'humour' hypocrite—leaves the novel while being seen as extremely, and genuinely *nasty*. Compare Uriah Heep. Dickens's vision is hard and straight. It is often cruel. And Pumblechook is not a genial creation. This consideration—a question at this point—may lead the pupil to a view of Dickens's grotesqueries more complex, and therefore more interesting, than a simple funny/not funny reaction could ever be. And the point is easy to make. To put it in an extreme way: the tough seriousness of a reader intent on serious fiction may be

Teaching Fiction in Schools

abashed by the even tougher humours of our warm-hearted Victorian entertainer.

This may be true of the comedy. But how do we approach the novel as a whole?

The problem, as always in Dickens and for readers of any age, is to clarify *in a satisfying way* at what distance, or gradation of distance, from reality the fiction demands to be taken. The assumption—all too easy in reading books called novels—that Dickens is a realistic (or 'naturalistic'?) writer like George Eliot is fatal. It accounts on the one hand for an uneasy dismissal of him as a caricaturist, and on the other for a somewhat forced defence on the lines of Santayana's challenge (quoted by Dr Leavis) that, 'When people say that Dickens exaggerates, it seems to me that they can have no eyes and no ears.' It accounts also, unfortunately, for the fairly recent, and massive, elevation of him as a kind of by-product of the Shakespeare Industry: a writer whose 'symbolic texture' is what we should (having missed it for a century) latch on to.

The truth is, no doubt, a mixture—a variable mixture. But one has, willy-nilly, to try to define the precise nature of one's own response in reading the novels—above all before introducing them to pupils. We shall therefore now suggest one approach which might reconcile those who find Dickens entertaining but (on the level of consciousness at least) not sufficiently serious; those who find him a frothy bore; those who find him a portentous bore; and those, if any, who immediately feel themselves in the presence of a great and fully serious writer.

Admittedly *Great Expectations* is, as we remarked earlier, more like ordinary novels than are most of Dickens's works. Apart from the relatively high degree of discipline applied to the grotesque and humorous elements, there are few readers who will not admit Pip to be a quite, or even very, credible 'psychological portrait'. He is unusual in Dickens not because he seems right at any one moment, but because he *develops* in a satisfactory manner. We find it easy to admit as lifelike the changes from the bullied child, to the spoilt 'gentleman', to the chastened and modestly industrious Gentleman. This is the obvious course of the book, and we do not feel embarrassed by it as we do by, for example, the courses of Martin Chuzzlewit or David Copperfield. Pip will 'do' in an average kind of way, in spite of the passages of inspired insight and the passages of uninspired falsity which accompany his progress. But, and this is crucial in reading Dickens in general, even the acceptable Pip is certainly not acceptable as the *substance* of a novel with claims to great distinction. If we were, intent on justification, talking simply of a 'psychological portrait' we should have to remark that most competent novelists could do *most* of Pip's experience. While comparison with George Eliot would reveal a colossal banality, even Trollope could be shown to be superior in this respect. The greatness of the novel lies elsewhere.

It does not lie, as it occasionally does in Dickens, in a brilliant excrescence of creation at the fringes. It lies, we feel, in a *pattern*, an impressive coherence of a complex set of 'characters', incidents and language, which the reader insensibly comes to perceive. It is this, composed mainly of the actions of fixed figures with no pretension to psychological development, which is the real substance of the book. To assert that its components do or do not resemble people round the corner is about as relevant as complaining that actors on Radio always sound like actors, or that people in Opera quite unnaturistically sing. What matters is the validity of the pattern. It makes *Great Expectations* very much more than Pip's story: and it is therefore to this that the pupil should be adverted.

To defend these views we shall: (A) provide a schematised, and thus crude, account of this pattern; and, (B) indicate some questions which may help the pupil to realise it *critically* for himself. We hope that the result will be to suggest that the novel is one of the most profound as well as one of the most interestingly questionable in English.

Teaching Fiction in Schools

(A) The book seems to us to explore at some depth the relations of parts of the human being to each other (and, by implication, the parts of society to each other), and to emphasise dramatically that these parts must come *into* relation. Pip's rise in fortune (and consequent snubbing or evasion of his past) is thus not a simple study in snobbery, but part of an image of dissociation (internal and external) between parts of the psyche, which must *be* resolved. And the means employed to make this image are not primarily those of the analysis in depth of any one person, least of all Pip, but the manipulation of the *relations* between a number of representative people who are relatively simply sketched in.

We are not, of course, denying that the novel is also a superb portrait of, and withering criticism about, some aspects of Victorian England. This is obvious. But it does nevertheless seem that there are two extremes between which the action flows: the coarse, violent, brutal, stupid, and sensual world of Magwitch, Orlick, and Bentley Drummle—which Pip almost hysterically denies. And the beautiful, corrupt, rich, genteel, and icy dream world of Miss Havisham and Estella—to which he so fervently aspires.* *Neither* of these worlds—or poles—is properly human; and neither, so it transpires, can become so except in intimate contact with the other.

The confrontation is treated in a great variety of ways, all rich with implication and association. Out of many examples we shall take two: they are deliberately chosen as peripheral to the main action, in order to illustrate the pervasiveness of the unifying inspiration of the book. Consider first the case of Mrs Joe Gargery. She is a debased and psychically cramped representative of respectability, education, and getting on in the world. She resents being married to a blacksmith. She makes virtue sour because of her

---

* Consider the implications in the names: of Orlick who calls himself 'Old' even though he is young and may suggest the 'old Adam'; of Estella, the remote and cold star, characteristically covered in jewels.

ignorance of its relation to feeling, of anything but its provincial externals. It is she who wishes to gain a foothold with Miss Havisham through the hitherto useless Pip. But then into her world comes the sudden eruption of a savage brutality:

> Nothing had been taken away from any part of the house. Neither, beyond the blowing out of a candle—which stood on a table between the door and my sister, and was behind her when she stood facing the fire and was struck—was there any disarrangement of the kitchen, excepting such as she herself had made, in falling and bleeding. But there was one remarkable piece of evidence on the spot. She had been struck with something blunt and heavy, on the head and spine; after the blows were dealt, something heavy had been thrown down at her with considerable violence, as she lay on her face. And on the ground beside her, when Joe picked her up, was a convict's leg-iron which had been filed asunder. (Chapter XVI.)

This we suspect—and later learn—is the act of the unregenerate Orlick, and the weapon a potent reminder of the marshes, and convict ships, and Pip's first encounter with Magwitch: all that she, and in a different but related way Pip, most want to shut out of consciousness. As it stands the picture is a marvellous example of Dickens's cruel and bizarre imagination, comparable in some detail to the passionate fire which later destroys Miss Havisham. But it is not left to stand by itself. There follows one of the most striking, and at first sight puzzling, episodes in the book: the human wreck left as a result of the crime wishes to see her destroyer, whom she can only indicate by the sign of a hammer (it is with a hammer that Orlick is later to attempt Pip's murder):

> Orlick, without a doubt! She had lost his name, and could only signify him by his hammer. We told him why

we wanted him to come into the kitchen, and he slowly laid down his hammer, wiped his brow with his arm, took another wipe at it with his apron, and came slouching out, with a curious loose vagabond bend in the knees that strongly distinguished him.

I confess that I expected to see my sister denounce him, and that I was disappointed by the different result. She manifested the greatest anxiety to be on good terms with him, evidently much pleased by his being at length produced, and motioned that she would have him given something to drink. She watched his countenance as if she were particularly wishful to be assured that he took kindly to his reception, she showed every possible desire to conciliate him, and there was an air of humble propitiation in all she did, such as I have seen pervade the bearing of a child towards a hard master. After that day, a day rarely passed without her drawing the hammer on her slate, and without Orlick's slouching in and standing doggedly before her, as if he knew no more than I did what to make of it. (Chapter XVI.)

It seems that, having lost everything, Mrs Joe has regained the capacity to feel, and possibly to forgive. The latter is, of course, confirmed in her (tear-jerking) dying words. But at this point the episode stands bare. *Psychologically* it would only make sense if she realised that Orlick attacked her (which goes against the evidence); and such a realisation would involve questions as to whether she is still frightened of him or perversely worships him, etc. But in *reading* these questions are mute. Dickens directs attention away from such enquiry for very good reasons: the incident, leg-iron and all, is a powerful *figure* scarcely involving real, complex, George Eliot humanity. It is created solely as a grotesque and disturbing symbol of the violent necessity to connect the ideal and the brutal which is the book's main theme.

Another example, but entirely different: two of the dominating persons in Pip's London are Jaggers and

Wemmick. They carry on a legal business (Jaggers would challenge anyone who hinted that it was not legal!) which relies entirely on suppressing fellow feeling and on not admitting anything—Jaggers's conversational style is only the most obvious example of this. Yet the case of the latter, Wemmick, is made *very* clear by Dickens. His home life is an idyll with the Aged Parent and Miss Skiffins, which shows him as full of bourgeois and Dickensian warmth and decency. But this is in itself a tiny, parodistic, figure of dissociation in the shape of the ludicrous castle (an Englishman's 'home is his castle' is a phrase actually used in the novel) which cuts off the decencies he is supposed to represent from contact with the outside world of Newgate and the Law.

Jaggers is at once subtler, more potent, and less sympathetic. One of the first things Pip notices about him is the perfume on his hands. Then, when we have before us the full force of his relation with sordid criminality—the combination of a domineering position with the refusal to admit that he is personally involved—the significance of the perfume is made plain:

> It fell out as Wemmick had told me it would, that I had an early opportunity of comparing my guardian's establishment with that of his cashier and clerk. My guardian was in his room, washing his hands with scented soap, when I went into the office from Walworth; and he called me to him, and gave me the invitation for myself and friends which Wemmick had prepared me to receive. 'No ceremony,' he stipulated, 'and no dinner dress, and say to-morrow.' I asked him where we should come to (for I had no idea where he lived), and I believe it was in his general objection to make anything like an admission, that he replied, 'Come here, and I'll take you home with me.' I embrace this opportunity of remarking that he washed his clients off, as if he were a surgeon or a dentist. He had a closet in his room, fitted up for the purpose,

which smelt of the scented soap like a perfumer's shop. It had an unusually large jack-towel on a roller inside the door, and he would wash his hands, and wipe them and dry them all over this towel, whenever he came in from a police-court or dismissed a client from his room. When I and my friends repaired to him at six o'clock next day, he seemed to have been engaged on a case of a darker complexion than usual, for, we found him with his head butted into this closet, not only washing his hands, but laving his face and gargling his throat. And even when he had done all that, and had gone all round the jack-towel, he took out his penknife and scraped the case out of his nails before he put his coat on.

There were some people slinking about as usual when we passed out into the street, who were evidently anxious to speak with him; but there was something so conclusive in the halo of scented soap which encircled his presence, that they gave it up for that day. As he walked along westward, he was recognised ever and again by some face in the crowd of the streets, and whenever that happened he talked louder to me; but he never otherwise recognised anybody, or took notice that anybody recognised him.

He conducted us to Gerrard Street, Soho . . . (Chapter XXVI.)

Why does Pip digress into—or, rather, 'embrace this opportunity' to give—a detailed account of Jagger's lavatorial habits? Why does he let fall the brilliantly casual pun on 'case'? Freud apart (and we believe that he would wish to be apart) the passage is at once a most suggestive symbol of Jaggers's refusal to involve himself in the meanness and squalor of other people *and* an implication that there is something in him which is revolted by what his life is. The reader is positively *pushed* into a reference to Pontius Pilate: a reference to the odd relationship between what people do and what they really think, in their private selves, of what they do—with the dramatic concomitant of the

Great Expectations

ineffectual, and constantly repeated, ritual of washing the hands.

This way of presentation is essential to Dickens's main purposes in *Great Expectations*. These 'symbolic' situations and acts, rather than the more explicit lines of the action, form the substance of the book. And they have a place in a pattern which we may now outline: if one recognises the relation between the extremes of brute nature and cold dream—the all too real and the ideal—as the poles between which the main action flows, then one perceives a very definite, and beautiful, coherence. This is not tidy, since the novel *is* semi-naturalistic and not an allegory. But it is felt by the reader—perhaps all the more for a few lifelike and unruly touches. To put it briefly: Pip has to learn that the Expectations which allow and promote his 'unhappy' aspirations towards Estella are in fact rooted in that very brute and criminal nature that he most wants to banish from consciousness and from his society. They derive from Magwitch—with all his savage lack of social grace and his coarsely direct and absolute love. At first this appalls all Pip's insulating decencies. But he then has to witness Estella, because of *her* deficiencies, giving herself to the seemingly similar (but by no means identical) coarseness and brutality of Bentley Drummle. This is, significantly, the action which brings Miss Havisham to some sense of the humanity she has repressed: she still has feeling enough to be horrified by the choice made by her own creation. Further, Pip has to come to sympathise with, even love and respect, Magwitch; recognising the humanity in the brutality from which the Expectations sprung, and discovering that Estella herself is the daughter of Magwitch and Molly-the-Murderess. (What a Victorian plot, and what a blow against chromosomes!—but with a purpose.) In Magwitch there is an ideal—Pip as a Gentleman—just as fantastic and unworldly and uncoarse as anything in the Havisham *ménage*. The situation is tangled and complex and compromised. The extremes become perplexing identities. And the recognition of all this leads Pip to that fever which is so often in Dickens, and elsewhere, the sign of a change of heart. When it is over Pip is equipped to recognise realities as opposed to Expectations. He is given by the novel a relatively modest job, and is able to *feel* the virtues of Joe and Biddy as opposed to merely seeing them with a rather shame-faced part of himself. He still has to face his deserved disappointments. But finally (in Dickens's second and softened ending, which to our minds is *by far the best* on every ground) he can meet again the ideal Estella who is herself chastened and brought to some kind of humanity by her contact with the beastly Drummle—'he either beats or cringes' said the complacently wise Jaggers (and he beat). Then they can perhaps start on a life which is neither brutalised nor coldly ideal, but much reduced in youth and pretension. Perhaps: it seems to us no coincidence that the last lines, with their mournful hopefulness, deliberately echo, as well as previous departures in the novel, Milton's description of the departure of Adam and Eve from Paradise. Comparison of the passages will confirm this.

Such a scheme may seem too neat and too partial. But it does at least suggest the ways in which we feel the organisation of Dickens's novels as related to, but importantly different from, the predominantly naturalistic form normally associated with the Novel. His work is within that form, but it is at the borders: his vision is less conscious, less analytic, than that of most novelists, but not less intelligent. And this perhaps accounts for his great hold on some readers, *and* for the distrust with which the determinedly serious often view him.

(B) To suggest such views to a class, all kinds of questions —relevant to the compact interrelatedness of the work and its precise distance from 'reality'—might be asked. We shall list only a few.

(1) Perhaps the most permanent and permeating question in the novel is 'Who is talking?' at any one point. In a story

told by an older and wiser man about himself, by an author who is neither, this has more than a tiresome 'technical' interest. It may help, for example, the many readers who rebel against the snobbish repugnance felt by both Pip and the impeccable Herbert in the crucial scenes after Magwitch's return from Australia. Their attitude *is* decidedly unpleasant, particularly in the eyes of the victim of twentieth-century enlightenment. But *whose* is it? If the book was not written in the first person the author might well explicitly endorse or dismiss it. As it is we have, reluctantly, to think for ourselves. Certainly the narrator, the elder Pip, seems to find the young gentlemen's attitudes quite natural (see, especially, Chapter XLI). There is a definite warmth—some might say a Dickensian warmth—in passages like

> 'I might have gone [for a soldier], my dear Herbert, but for the prospect of taking counsel with your friendship and affection'.
> Of course I broke down there: and of course Herbert, beyond seizing a warm grip of my hand, pretended not to notice . . ., etc.

Good old Herbert. But why the cosy/manly 'of course'? The attitude is repulsive: is it the author's as well as the narrator's? Is the *novel* behind this piddling and mechanical 'gentleman' morality? In the long run it obviously is not, as is shown by Pip's eventual loyalty to Magwitch (which nevertheless requires a curious 'softening' in the Warmint). But the critically alert reader—in this case the reader who is enquiring ‚who is talking?'—should not have to go so far to find where Dickens stands. He should *immediately* perceive that, by means of the very next chapter—Magwitch's life-story told in his devastatingly healthy prose—the young gentlemen are dramatically 'placed', and very firmly placed. Such points may seem obvious. That they are not always so, even to the brilliant enthusiast, is indicated by Bernard Shaw's seemingly formidable challenge:

If Pip had no objection to be a parasite instead of an honest blacksmith, at least he had a better claim to be a parasite on Magwitch's earnings than, as he imagined, on Miss Havisham's property. *It is curious that this should not have occurred to Dickens* . . . (our italics).

Clearly Shaw is here a victim to the elder Pip's voice. For the novel is concerned *throughout* to show the inescapable relation (*mixture* is perhaps a better word) between the refined world and the brutal one, whether these are sources of income or people. One wonders whether a reader like Shaw—misled as he may have been by other of Dickens's books where the imagination does not force its way through the current assumptions, and real social pressures, about Gentlemen, etc.—could appreciate the most delightfully savage irony of *Great Expectations*, on which we have already touched. That the powerfully 'low' Magwitch is himself the most class-conscious personage, the greatest admirer of 'parasites', and the biggest snob of all.

Pip—and I am afraid Pip must be to this extent identified with Dickens—could not see Magwitch as an animal of the same species as himself or Miss Havisham. His feeling is true to the nature of snobbery; but his creator says no word in criticism of that ephemeral limitation.

'Ephemeral limitation' is generous: but Shaw's '*says no word*' is a horrid warning about how not to read a novel of this kind. And, as we have suggested, the way to avoid such mistakes is to ask the relevant, literary critical, questions.

A further advantage of being alert to the 'voice' of the novel is that the reader is better able to judge where and why it really fails. This is rarely, in our opinion; but when it does happen it is correspondingly more disastrous, and thus more educative about the reading of fiction, than if we were to take a simple view of the narration. There are occasions when the authorial presence is insufficient to counteract the

Great Expectations

Pip/elder Pip tone. When, for instance, Joe first comes to London and behaves in the face of his own and Pip's embarrassment with great distinction (Chapter XXVII) we are treated to this reflection: 'I had not been mistaken in my fancy that there was a simple dignity in him'. The trouble with this is that, for all our dislike of the complacency indicated by the words 'fancy' and 'simple' the judgement is sufficiently *close* to our response to be acceptable. It receives little dramatic contradiction because it needs little: but the diction *jars*. More seriously, and very differently, the whole episode of Pip's initial parting with Biddy and Joe walks a dramatic tightrope. Before the Expectations appear Pip and Biddy have this conversation:

> 'Joe and I would perhaps have gone partners when I was out of my time, and I might even have grown up to keep company with you, and we might have sat on this very bank on a fine Sunday, quite different people. I should have been good enough for *you*; shouldn't I, Biddy?'
>
> Biddy sighed as she looked at the ships sailing on, and returned for answer, 'Yes; *I* am not over-particular.' It scarcely sounded flattering, but I knew she meant well. (Chapter XVII.)

Here it is clear that we are *not* supposed to sympathise with the intolerably patronising, Estella worshipping, Pip: we and the elder Pip see more than he does. On the other hand we may feel inclined to revolt against the authorial control, or, rather, its lack of tact. After all no candid, as opposed to resolutely socialist, reader is likely to wish Pip's wishes out of the way entirely (this is a story), and in this scene the author is savaging them prematurely.

(2) Other points about the great question of Gentility could be made less 'technical' and more general. 'What is a Gentleman in this novel?' Such a question reveals all kinds of curious interrelations and contrasts. Undoubtedly Bentley Drummle is a gentleman—in a way. But then in other ways

he is more akin to Orlick than he is to Matthew and Herbert Pocket. And they, in their turn, are curiously ineffectual in spite of being very definitely the genuine article, and in spite of Pip's late revised estimate of Herbert's capacity for success in business. Then what about Compeyson? And why is the only gentleman who is strong, genuine, *and* decent, the shadowy Startop? Like the questioning of the narrator's voice these considerations tend to cut through a simple reading of the novel as an unanalysed attack on snobbery, and to produce a wilderness of mirrors. The teacher will be able to think of much more.

(3) To revert briefly to the language of the novel. It is easy to point to the extraordinary verbal imagination of Dickens, either as a way of generating enthusiasm or of rationalising it. In *Great Expectations* the teacher has only to ask a few questions of the type, 'What is it in Chapter XI that establishes Sarah Pocket, Raymond, and Camilla as legacy-hungry hypocrites without the author actually *telling* us what they are?' 'What makes the strange man in the *Jolly Bargemen* in Chapter X so striking—is it his habit of looking "as if he were taking aim at something with an invisible gun"?' 'Why do we feel that a convict's leg-iron or a Havisham jewel are more significant objects than Pip's socks?'—or, in a more sophisticated formulation—'Does Dickens let his "symbols" grow out of the natural habitat as opposed to imposing them into it from outside?' 'What, similarly, is the point of our often being reminded of Joe's discomfort in Sunday or town clothes and of his eventual rejection of them—is it simply that they itch and are a poor fit?' 'What makes Orlick's attack on Pip in Chapter LIII more convincing than the mere melodrama referred to by some critics? Has it anything to do with Pip's surreal vision of what it would be like for him to be dead while Orlick was alive: "My rapid mind pursued him to the town, made a picture of the street with him in it, and contrasted its lights and life with the lonely marsh and the white vapour creeping over it, into which I should have dissolved."?' '*Why* is it that

Great Expectations

Wemmick's bland description of the cast of a hanged man "... it's the genuine look. Much as if one nostril was caught up with a horse-hair and a little fish-hook" is so telling?'

These are, we repeat, only a few of the facets which could be mentioned in eliciting a truly critical response to the novel.

(4) There are points in *Great Expectations* where it is possible to isolate very definitely the 'distance from reality' at which Dickens has chosen to work. Pip says that Bill Barley 'had but to stick to his pepper and rum' to die conveniently for everyone except (presumably) himself (Chapter LII). And we are not invited to have any response to Bill except as a conveniently comic obstacle. Yet the attitude does not, in this case, jar at all. The question is not 'What does Bill Barley feel about dying?', but 'Why is Pip's remark not felt as appallingly callous?'. And the answer tells us a lot about what (in a qualified sense) we might call Dickens's 'characterisation'—compare, again, George Eliot. Similarly, 'How much does it matter that an ignorant blacksmith and a notably deprived blacksmith's boy should, in Chapter VII, display such fine and correct feelings towards women (in the unglamorous person of Mrs Joe), such a delicate and even high falutin' morality?' The answer is that it matters not at all: but the question illuminates the relationship between Dickens and a strict 'realism'. It helps us to see the nature of the convention within which *Great Expectations* was written and demands to be read.

(5) Finally there are questions which could provide a channel and relief for any hostility to the book which is not resolved by discussion of its tone. If Miss Havisham is felt by a pupil (as she might well be) to be too melodramatic a personage-with-properties, then a distinction could be attempted between the genuine and frightening oddness registered by Pip as a child and the Grand Guignol of some (and only some) of the later scenes—the 'love her, love her, love her' of Chapter XXIX, for example. And this distinction might be furthered and sharpened by a suggested com-

parison between Miss Havisham and her properties and Jaggers and his. Jaggers, compared to her, possesses an *active* life and menace—where is this evident?

Again there is the curious episode (Chapter LI) in which the ruthless efficiency of Jaggers breaks down into some rather vague 'Victorian' hints about having felt the tender passion. Admittedly this is clearly a designed parallel to the similar, but far less comforting, breakdown of Miss Havisham upon Pip's avowal of his maniacal love for Estella, but it *seems* a weak point in the creation. Dickens tries to cover it up with . . . what?—with the famous cross-examination style and with Jaggers's and Wemmick's subsequent, relieved, brutality to Mike. But it does not at all cohere with the Jaggers we have been so powerfully and confidently shown. Nor, and this is the point, does it bear any but a very forced relationship to the main themes of the book. Or does it? Here we have a perfect opportunity for the development of the critical capacity. Should the reader (as we do) feel that Dickens is giving in to a sentimental assertion of the solidarity of mankind as *really* having decent feelings in spite of satisfyingly cruel and frightening appearances? Or is he, as he has already done with Wemmick, convincingly reinforcing his dramatisation of the necessary coherence, precariously achieved, of the psyche? In short: *The way to approach Dickens is to persist in questions of this kind.*

There are many other questions, on all levels. 'Are the (Matthew) Pockets somewhat forced and overdone?' 'Why is Pip's love for Estella such an absolute thing, especially since she herself scarcely exists as a character, at whatever distance from reality we take her?' 'What is the point of Pip's being instrumental in the dismissal of both Orlick and Trabb's Boy?' But to suggest answers to these would be to insult the intelligence of the reader. All we hope to have done is to hint at one way of looking at the novel, and of persuading others to look at it.

9

PRIDE AND PREJUDICE

'IT IS a truth universally acknowledged, that a single man in possession of a good fortune must be in want of a wife.' Whatever the pleasure with which, on another occasion, he may have greeted the opening sentence of *Pride and Prejudice*, the teacher of English is bound to view it with misgivings when it presents itself in the company of a class of fifteen-year-old adolescents. The obstacle it presents is not that it describes a state of affairs that lies outside their experience. That, in itself, could be an advantage. Nor is it that they cannot understand it. They probably can. The trouble is simply that they do not regard the remark as worth making, and it will not help to point out to them that the kind of people it criticises is a kind they themselves might want to criticise—people who cannot mind their own business. In all likelihood the reply would be that the same kind of people enjoy such remarks—people who have nothing more interesting to do than pride themselves on their superiority.

Meeting Elizabeth Bennet soon convinces them that this is not just a story about stuffy people for stuffy people, but their sympathy with her is of little help if it leads to a reading of the novel as an account of laughing Lizzy, ably aided and abetted by her wise-cracking pa, challenging and routing the forces of convention. It is easy enough for a young reader to share Elizabeth's feelings when Mr Collins proposes to her, when Charlotte disappoints her or when Lady Catherine tries to put her in her place. It is a very different matter when such a reader tries to understand what the heroine is going on about, when she warns her father:

> Our importance, our respectability in the world must be affected by the wild volatility, the assurance and disdain of all restraint which mark Lydia's character. Excuse me, for I must speak plainly. If you, my dear father, will not take the trouble of checking her exuberant spirits, and of teaching her that her present pursuits are not to be the business of her life, she will soon be beyond the reach of amendment.

And despite the simplicity of the feeling it is even harder when such a reader encounters a passage like:

> 'But can you think that Lydia is so lost to everything but love of him as to live with him on any other terms than marriage?'
> 'It does seem, and it is most shocking indeed,' replied Elizabeth, with tears in her eyes, 'that a sister's sense of decency and virtue in such a point should admit of doubt. But, really, I know not what to say. Perhaps I am not doing her justice. But she is very young . . .'

Nevertheless, while it may be impossible and perhaps even undesirable for our pupils to share the sense of decorum which informs such utterances, unless they can at least learn to appreciate that sense of decorum there is no point in reading Jane Austen with them.

Unfortunately it is easy to read *Pride and Prejudice*—or rather to mis-read it—with considerable enjoyment but with no appreciation whatever of decorum, up to the point where it suddenly becomes apparent that Elizabeth and Mr Bennet have both been guilty of grave errors. To the reader with a sense of decorum, of course, those errors have been

Pride and Prejudice

evident all along, but to a reader not so blessed the first half of the book might suggest that shafts of wit are all the equipment required by a pilgrim along life's way. These shafts, of course, obligingly fall in showers for which, unquestionably, we must all be grateful, especially those of us who teach. The book, however, must not be treated as a display of fireworks, because Jane Austen's wit, unlike that of Oscar Wilde, does not display itself in a series of isolatable witticisms. Wherever she employs her wit, it *tells*.

Returning to Chapter I, take for example Mr Bennet's ironical assurance to his wife—'I have a great respect for your nerves. They are my old friends. I have heard you mention them with consideration these twenty years at least.' Taken in isolation this remark would justify Fowler's charge that the aim of irony is, by the use of double-talk, to foster a flattering sense of belonging to an inner circle—that sense of superiority which, although like our pupils we find it damnable in others, we occasionally indulge in ourselves, as, possibly, when we find an application for Mr Bennet's formula among our own acquaintance. His words, indeed, verge on sarcasm, the aim of which is not even the gratification of a sense of superiority but the infliction of pain. For these faults the novelist has a punishment in store for Mr Bennet if not for us. She is content for us to be amused by the remark because its victim is a fictitious character who embodies weaknesses that merit ridicule. (Elizabeth and Mr Darcy discuss the ethics of ridicule most lucidly in Chapter XI.) As the novelist plainly (not ironically) informs us about Mrs Bennet, in endorsement of the truth if not the propriety of her husband's remark, 'when she was discontented she fancied herself nervous'. The most characteristic feature of her behaviour is a total disregard for the wishes of anybody except herself, and it is on this that the wit fastens. Appreciation of Jane Austen's wit, therefore, misses her point unless it is guided by a sense of propriety like that which prompts Elizabeth's reproof of her father, quoted earlier, totally lacking though it be in entertainment value.

The wit does not scoff at decorum. On the contrary, it reinforces it. At the risk of being a wet blanket, the teacher should therefore ask his pupils what sort of a husband would talk to his wife like that in front of their children.

If we divide the characters into two groups—those, like Jane Bennet, Colonel Fitzwilliam, the Gardiners, and Mr Darcy, who can be relied on, and those like Charlotte Lucas, Mr Wickham and—alas—Mr Bingley, who can not, it is clear that Mr Bennet belongs in the second group no less than his wife does. The difference is that while her infirmity renders her as vulnerable to ridicule as those other monsters of egotism, Lady Catherine and Mr Collins, he has paid more attention to his defences.

> To his wife he was very little otherwise indebted, than as her ignorance and folly had contributed to his amusement. This is not the sort of happiness which a man would in general wish to owe to his wife; but where other powers of entertainment are wanting, the true philosopher will derive benefit from such as are given.

A class will quickly perceive that Jane Austen shares their hostility towards superior people. It is sufficiently evident, for example, in her early account of the Bingley sisters.

> They are rather handsome, had been educated in one of the first private seminaries in town, had a fortune of twenty thousand pounds, were in the habit of spending more than they ought, and of associating with people of rank; and were therefore in every respect entitled to think well of themselves, and meanly of others.

Also sufficiently evident is the irony of this account. The task is to perceive the irony in the account of Mr Bennet, 'the true philosopher', and to admit that, amusing though his observations may be, he too belongs in the ranks of self-conscious superiority. Among other critical achievements, this calls for a distinction between Mr Bennet's cynical wit and the normative wit of the novel. There are places where the gap between the two becomes very noticeable indeed, as in Chapter XLI, where, in answer to Elizabeth's warning that Lydia's behaviour is of great 'disadvantage' to the family, Mr Bennet enquires of his favourite daughter: 'What, has she frightened away some of your lovers? Poor little Lizzy! But do not be cast down.' It is not that the heroine is sacrosanct. When she behaves improperly she is no less open to mockery than the other characters—as when, in Chapter XXIV, we are told that as she saw more of Mr Wickham, 'to his other recommendations was now added that of general unreserve'. (Later, when she remorsefully reviewed this period of her life, and remembered Wickham's confidences— 'She was *now* struck with the impropriety of such communications to a stranger, and wondered it had escaped her before.') The difference between Mr Bennet's wit and that of his creator is one of truthfulness and tone. Apart from this, he does not expose himself. He cannot be the butt of the kind of wit he turns on his wife. It is not until the second half of the book, where responsibility shows up more than charm, that an event unambiguously reveals his past deficiencies.

The event in question, Lydia's elopement, constitutes an impropriety which it is even harder for our pupils to perceive as such than Mr Bennet's wit. Lydia is a character with whom they feel completely at home. While they are not insensitive to indications in the writing that the novelist disapproves of her, their first impulse is to treat these indications as signs of prudishness in the novelist.

> She had high animal spirits, and a sort of natural self-consequence, which the attention of the officers, to whom her uncle's good dinners and her own easy manners recommended her, had increased into assurance. She was very equal, therefore, to address Mr Bingley on the subject

of the ball, and abruptly reminded him of his promise...

Good for her!

> All were struck with the stranger's air, all wondered who he could be; and Kitty and Lydia, determined if possible to find out, led the way across the street, under pretence of wanting something in an opposite shop, and fortunately had just gained the pavement when the two gentlemen, turning back, had reached the same spot.

Nice work! Surely you're not going to pretend there's anything wrong in that?

At such a juncture it is both hopeless and unwarrantable to tell our pupils that they are in some sense 'wrong', and, this being so, might the best policy with *Pride and Prejudice* be, after all, to leave it alone unless it is required reading for examination purposes? Now there is only one good reason for not trying a good novel with a class, and that is the belief that, even when they have got well into it, they will not want to go on to the end. On this ground, and this ground only, it may be best not to venture on *Pride and Prejudice* with a class of boys. Even if they think that Jane Austen does not know what she is talking about, however, a class of girls will want to go on to the end. They will become involved with Elizabeth, not merely in her scintillating moments, but even more in her mortification when she realises how she has wronged Mr Darcy, and her purgatory when she realises that she loves him. The delicacy of this sympathy in itself shows that we are not reduced to reading the novel with a room full of Lydias. Even if we were, however, it would be profitable to go along with them to see what they could learn from the experience, though it might not be all that we would desire. What can they learn from Lydia that will help them to appreciate decorum?

A conspicuous part of Lydia's indecorum is her lack of common prudence. This might seem an unpromising point at which to engage the critical attention of the teen-age reader, but in fact youthful contempt for worldly considerations is largely conventional. It is at this point more than at any other that our pupils are likely to be guilty of affectation, pretending innocence of anxieties which actually disturb them considerably. Part of their contempt for the novel's opening sentence stems from this source. What does it matter whether a man is of 'good fortune' or not—that Mr Bingley, for example, is 'worth' four or five thousand a year?

This question should not be allowed to pass as rhetorical. Given a hint that the question is not closed, a class needs no encouragement to consider it seriously. The novel offers no hard and fast answer. When a man like Mr Collins proposes marriage, the fact that he is heir to Longbourn carries no weight at all. Nevertheless, financial statements are worthy of some attention because they have human consequences. For example—

> Mr Bennet's property consisted almost entirely in an estate of two thousand a year, which, unfortunately for his daughters, was entailed, in default of heirs male, on a distant relation; and their mother's fortune, though ample for her situation in life, could but ill supply the deficiency of his. Her father had been an attorney in Meryton, and had left her four thousand pounds.

Elizabeth herself becomes bitterly but objectively aware of the unfortunate implications for the daughters, when she is deserted by Mr Wickham for a dull heiress because 'handsome young men must have something to live on'. There are also implications for the parents, as the mother continually reminds everybody, and the father is forced to admit when he has no funds available to salvage Lydia from the wreck into which she imprudently steers.

There are, admittedly, features of *Pride and Prejudice* which require the kind of explanation which begins, 'Well, in *those* days'. Attitudes to the adventure of running away from home have certainly changed, so that trying to get a class to understand the shock and sympathise with the distress occasioned to her family by Lydia's elopement involves inviting them to an effort of historical imagination. Getting them to see that she has made a fool of herself, however, does not. 'Thoughtless, thoughtless Lydia!' is Elizabeth's cry, on reading her sister's announcement of what she has done, that begins, 'You will laugh when you know where I am gone.' There is no obstacle to a modern reader's sharing at least in that response, and by the end of the book a girl reader, at any rate, may not dismiss as utterly feeble Jane's protest when her father jokingly foretells that she and Bingley, when married, will always exceed their income. 'Imprudence or thoughtlessness in money matters would be unpardonable in *me*.' She may, that is, agree—not submissively but realistically.

This is one surprising discovery which *Pride and Prejudice* has to offer a young reader—that some of the precepts of decency (to give it a more modern name) are not irrational taboos but are based on hard experience of the kind that reaches its appropriate finale in a legal settlement. Decorum, however, might seem inherently misplaced when it comes to experience of a softer quality. Can such experience find its appropriate finale in a paragraph like the following?

> Elizabeth, feeling all the more than common awkwardness and anxiety of his situation, now forced herself to speak; and immediately, though not very fluently, gave him to understand that her sentiments had undergone so material a change since the period to which he alluded, as to make her receive with gratitude and pleasure his present assurances. The happiness which this reply produced was such as he had probably never felt before; and he expressed himself on the occasion as sensibly and as warmly as a man violently in love can be supposed to do. Had Elizabeth been able to encounter his eyes, she

might have seen how well the expression of heartfelt delight diffused over his face became him; but, though she could not look, she could listen, and he told her of feelings which, in proving of what importance she was to him, made his affection every moment more valuable.

The restraint of this passage is not to be explained away in terms of irony. Irony is there, of course. The comic discrepancy between its succinct clarity and the confusion to which it refers, but which it makes no attempt to represent, is consistent and pointed. If that was all, however, this would be a case of Jane Austen's inviting us, with a maidenly twinkle, to guess the things the lovers actually mumbled. The tart final clause, evaluating Mr Darcy's feelings, excludes any such effect as that. What, then, is the point of the restraint? What is it, in fact, that is restrained? What is missing? The reader has been given all the information that he could have properly asked for if Elizabeth and Mr Darcy had been real people, and Jane Austen, of course, treats her characters with this same propriety throughout the narrative. It is not an example of inhibition, but of reserve.

The question of reserve is kept in sight throughout the book, from the moment Elizabeth and Charlotte, in Chapter VI, discuss Jane's neglect of every opportunity of inviting Mr Bingley's advances. It is distinguished sharply from coyness. Mr Darcy, for example, prefaces his second proposal of marriage with the remark, 'You are too generous to trifle with me', and when Mr Collins earlier attributes her refusal of *his* proposal to 'your wish of increasing my love by suspense, according to the usual practice of elegant females', she indignantly rejects all interest in that kind of elegance. 'I would rather be paid the compliment of being believed sincere.' What is abjured, in Jane Austen's reserve, is the attempt to coerce people.

There is sometimes, in addition, the factor of prudence. It was Lydia's lack of reserve that precipitated her misfortunes, and a similar lack in Miss Bingley exposes her to humiliating snubs from Mr Darcy, as at Netherfield, when, having pressed Elizabeth into walking up and down the room with her she invites him to join them, and then (against Elizabeth's advice) asks him to explain his reason for refusing. But reserve is not necessarily the policy of prudence. Charlotte Lucas finds prudential reasons why Jane 'should make the most of every half hour' she passes in Mr Bingley's company. 'When she is secure of him, there will be leisure for falling in love as much as she chooses'. Elizabeth herself never mentions the word 'love' in this discussion (Chapter VI), but her objections all imply its supreme relevance, not least when she warns her friend (in a remark which might just as well have been directed to her father): 'You make me laugh, Charlotte; but it is not sound.' The narrative completes the discussion when Charlotte practises what she preaches, and secures Mr Collins.

As this makes plain, reserve is a refusal to manipulate another person's feelings by a display of one's own. In courtship, clearly, this reticence cannot be proper in both sexes. Display, in one or the other of them, is essential. When the Gardiners observe Elizabeth and Mr Darcy together to make out whether they are in love—'Of the lady's sensations they remained a little in doubt; but that the gentleman was overflowing with admiration was evident enough.' In this scene, clearly, the expressive gentleman is no less to be commended than the inscrutable lady. What is most significant is not so much that Elizabeth does not betray her change of heart, but that her behaviour is in no way peculiar. Reserve—in the shape of a bashful or disdainful demeanour—can constitute a display of feeling as remarkable as any other, and no less harmful. For Jane Austen such reserve is either a constitutional weakness or else an offence (vide respectively the shy Miss Darcy and the cold Mrs Hurst, in Chapter XLV). True reserve is exhibited by Jane, who, when she was falling in love with Mr Bingley, 'united with great strength of feeling a composure of temper and a uniform cheerfulness of manner which would guard her from the suspicions of the impertinent.' In fact, to be true to itself reserved behaviour must be absolutely normal, because it consists in not going out of one's proper way in order to get one's own way.

Thus defined, the province of reserve extends far beyond the realm of romantic attachment, and the novel abounds in social scenes where it is cultivated by decent characters, who refrain from imposing on others, and neglected by aggressive characters, whose life-style is one of intrusion. But here again it relates especially to women, because in Jane Austen's world emotional display is the only weapon in the feminine armoury. Lady Catherine is the most prominent female bully, with Mrs Bennet a close second, but almost every woman is guilty, at one time or another, of bringing undue personal pressures to bear. In the early stages of the novel, for example, Elizabeth herself goes out of her way to attack Mr Darcy. Only Jane and Mrs Gardiner retain their integrity, in this respect, throughout. (Compare Mrs Gardiner's forbearance in making no attempt to '*force* her communication', when she wishes to discover the nature of the relationship between her niece and Mr Darcy, with the persistence of Miss Bingley in gratifying her own similar curiosity, when she '*forced* him to say what gave no one any pain but herself'—Chapters XLIV and XLV. Our italics.) It is surely instructive for our pupils to discover a moral perspective in which flirting and nagging appear in the same light.

To return to the question of romantic attachment, the objection which pupils commonly raise against reserve is that it is incompatible with deep feeling. Deep feeling, they believe, must declare itself or burst. No teacher of literature can afford to deny the existence of such compelling emotions. It is also worth pointing out, however, that Jane Austen too values deep feeling—feeling of a kind which is quite compatible with reserve because it can only be felt for a person one knows very well, and felt steadily. Thus, after Elizabeth has informed Mr Darcy of Lydia's disgrace, when he has left her, and she realises that she will probably never see him again, we are told:

> If gratitude and esteem are good foundations of affection, Elizabeth's change of sentiment will be thought neither improbable nor faulty. But if otherwise—if the regard springing from such sources is unreasonable or unnatural, in comparison of what is so often described as arising on a first interview with its object, and even before two words have been exchanged, nothing can be said in her defence, except that she had given somewhat of a trial to the latter method in her partiality for Wickham, and that its ill success might, perhaps, authorise her to seek the other less interesting mode of attachment. Be that as it may, she saw him go with regret. . . .

Deep feeling is something that has to grow naturally, and reserve is required to prevent the atmosphere of a drawing-room from turning into that of a hot-house. Thus, in Chapter VI, when Charlotte is urging that Jane should set her cap at Mr Bingley, she points out that these two have already spent four evenings together, 'and four evenings may do a great deal', to which Elizabeth replies:

> 'Yes; these four evenings have enabled them to ascertain that they both like Vingt-un better than Commerce; but with respect to any other leading characteristic, I do not imagine that much has been unfolded.'

Passages such as this might suggest that there is at least one sort of reserve in which both Elizabeth and Jane Austen are lacking, namely reserve in airing moral wisdom. But as regards fault-finding, it is worth noticing that Elizabeth comes to repent her one indulgence in recrimination, and that in general she does not pass a moral judgement unless it is invited or, as in the case of her advice to her father, called for. She does not revel in advertising her wisdom, as Mary does for example when Lydia elopes:

> 'Unhappy as the event must be for Lydia, we may draw from it this useful lesson: that loss of virtue in a female is irretrievable; that one false step involves her in endless ruin; that her reputation is no less brittle than it is beautiful; and that she cannot be too much guarded in her behaviour towards the undeserving of the other sex.'

Elizabeth lifted up her eyes in amazement, but was too much oppressed to make any reply.

As for Jane Austen, her most characteristic judgements are those which are most restrained in exactly the sense we have been discussing, lacking even the emphasis of understatement or irony. Here are two examples, taken from the description of the family life of the Bennets just after Lydia's marriage has been arranged. First, when the good news first breaks, and Mrs Bennet rises joyfully from her bed to preside at table: 'No sentiment of shame gave a damp to her triumph.' The other, when Lydia herself pays a visit, and as a married woman insists in sitting above Jane at table: 'It was not to be supposed that time would give Lydia that embarrassment from which she had been so wholly free at first.' Our plea has been that *Pride and Prejudice* deserves study because it calls certain current assumptions into question with intelligence and wit, but it is also well worth introducing those pupils who are capable of it to the pleasures offered by this kind of accuracy.

Perhaps, after all, our pupils are not unjustified in their suspicion that Jane Austen wrote for superior people. Where they go wrong is in being so sure they know what this involves. Superior people, it would seem, are distinguished not by airs and graces but by their good humour. Indeed, the basic moral of the tale is that with which Clarissa endows *The Rape of the Lock*:

Teaching Fiction in Schools

And trust me, dear! good-humour can prevail,
When airs, and flights, and screams, and scolding fail.

Dr Johnson's commendation of the utility of this precept is still valid.

10

DAUGHTERS OF THE VICAR

D. H. LAWRENCE's *Daughters of the Vicar* calls for a more developed reader than any of the other novels so far considered in this book. By this we do not mean a reader equipped with more considered experience of life: we mean a reader with more articulated experience of reading fiction. So much is implied by small details in the story. Indeed, it is not only experience of reading fiction which is required. Experience of poetry too is needed, to respond to the implications of a passage such as the following:

> In the dining-room was a small fire. Mrs Lindley, growing very stout, lay on her couch. The vicar carved the cold mutton: Miss Louisa, short and plump and rather flushed, came in from the kitchen; Miss Mary, dark, with a beautiful white brow and grey eyes, served the vegetables; the children chattered a little, but not exuberantly. The very air seemed starved.

Of course, all these details are realistic, but each detail also has a metaphorical force. The dining-room is the one room in the vicarage which is the scene of instinctive satisfactions, and the smallness of the fire indicates a poverty of instinctive life. In this context of famine, there is something monstrous in the grossness of the invalid Mrs Lindley. The details that the vicar carves and the mutton is cold are true-to-life, but also morally characteristic. So are the contrast in physical appearance between the two sisters, and even the facts (again completely plausible) that Louisa comes from the kitchen and Mary serves the vegetables (a virtuous and bloodless form of life). The subdued vivacity of the children links up with the sparseness of the fire, while the last sentence sums up the total impression in an image which is doubly forceful because of its context—starvation in the dining-room.

The poetic character of the writing does not, however, reside only in its metaphorical strength. Texture also is given significant play. Mrs Lindley—'s*tout* . . . *couch*'; 'the vicar *c*arved . . . *c*old; '*Lou*isa . . . p*l*ump . . . f*lu*shed'; Mary—'*b*eautiful . . . *b*row'; 'the *ch*ildren *ch*attered.' Such a density of effect is the product of an intense concern behind the writing. Each detail is like a pulse, in which the heart-beat of the story makes itself felt. The word 'heart' is less misleading than 'theme', because it cannot be mistaken as a metaphor for 'proposition', or 'moral', or 'subject'. Nevertheless, the word 'heart' is still misleading if it suggests something that can be plucked out, so that its connections with the various parts of the story can subsequently be anatomised in the classroom. What gives each detail significance is not its connection with some separable truth, but its connection with other details.

Towards the end of the first section of the story, for example, we are told how, when the collier children saw 'the pale distinguished procession' of the Lindley children pass by on their way to church, against their wills they felt inferior, 'and hate stirred their hearts'. This is a realistic detail, indicative of the Lindleys' situation at Aldecross. Before the end of the story has been reached, however, it pulses with moral implication as well. In the third section, for example, we find Louisa expressing an identical hatred of Mr Massy, because, against her will also, she must acknowledge his obviously superior virtue. The first detail,

Daughters of the Vicar

therefore, cannot be fully appreciated by the pupil who simply responds to it, as it stands, when he comes upon it. Because of its organic unity, the details of the story cannot be fully appreciated piecemeal, as and when they arise, but only in relation to each other. How is this difficulty to be dealt with by the teacher? The easiest way might seem to be to formulate the common underlying tension—as a conflict, say, between formality and vitality—and alert the pupil in advance to keep his eye open for instances. To do this, however, would be to kill the story. What is required is to read the story as it is written, in a series of overlapping waves. Start reading section by section. As one section succeeds another, invite backward glances at details from earlier sections which take on fresh significance in the light of details now presented. At the conclusion, appraise the story of its entirety, not by posing some central, all-embracing question, but by comparing analogous scenes, or by taking a single passage and enquiring why it contains the words it does.

The only pressure which the teacher needs exert is that necessary to prevent the mis-reading of the story as a stock romance of love over-leaping the barriers of social class. Class distinctions are, of course, convincingly presented. But class itself becomes, like the other realistic details, a metaphor. Indeed, it is almost a pun, once the philosophical meaning of the word 'class' is borne in mind. The inhumanity of the style of life represented by Mr Massy arises from its categorical obedience of abstract principles, and as Bertrand Russell (whom, in his idiosyncratic particulars Mr Massy so uncannily resembles) pointed out, such obedience, in essence, consists in the treatment of all instances of the same class in exactly the same way. This point—the subjection of personal relations to abstract relations—is made explicit by Lawrence in the concise fourth section. Indeed, part of the difficulty of the story is the intellectual demand it makes upon the reader. But, by the time he comes to this explicit section, the reader, like Louisa, should already have come to feel this point in his bones.

It is worth examining the reading which produces this feeling. An initial appraisal of the first section, describing the social position of the Lindleys at Aldecross, might concentrate on asking why Lawrence says that their education placed the children in the upper classes 'definitely and cruelly'. The difficulty of keeping up their 'superior position' is not merely financial. All sorts of hints are given as to the emotional aspects of the difficulty. An explanation might, for example, be sought for the insistence with which Lawrence stresses the difference between a rural parish and an industrial one, the detail with which he describes the vicarage building, and so on. The full nature of the difficulty of the 'superior position' only gradually becomes evident as the story proceeds. By the end of the first section, however, it is recognisably an artificial one, and therefore unhealthy, in which connection the pupil should be alerted to the images of pallor which run consistently through the story. Less obvious, but even more indicative of the dynamic of the narrative, is the image of a living thing that is half-protected, half imprisoned, by a brittle, shell-like form—an image offered in the first section not only by the diagnosis of Mrs Lindley's ailment ('unless she were careful, she would smash her form of life') but also by the description of the children in their Sunday-best clothes.

All this is plain sailing. More difficult is the cryptic statement that Louisa 'had more enemies than ideals'. The association of ideals with external shells is obvious enough, but the reference to hatred, although it is only one of several contained in this short passage, appears arbitrary. It must await a reading of the next section for its justification to become apparent. This second section continues to enrich the pattern already presented in the first. There are, for example, the mechanical nature of Mr Lindley's relations with his parishioners, Mrs Durant's complaint that the parish almanac is only in black and white, and the fact that old Mr Durant is just the shell of a man who had once been 'a great dancer and boxer'. The pattern is not, however,

Daughters of the Vicar

merely filled in. It is also extended, particularly by Mrs Durant's expression of her instinctive hatred of the life of traditional service, symbolised by her son's decision to join the Navy. 'He goes and makes a slave of himself, and he'll rue it.'

She herself is a slave to duty—family duty—and her obedience frets her. Mr Lindley's answering fury indicates a realisation that his own 'form of life' is under attack, and the fact that this makes him 'white at the gills' reminds us that pallor is not only a sign of anaemia. The references to suppressed hatred in the first section now fall clearly into place. The case of the Durants also reminds us that the problems of 'keeping up a position' are not confined to the upper classes, once the full significance of the word 'position' has been appreciated. The mutinous attitude of Louisa in the ensuing discussion at the Lindleys' luncheon-table shows that she has more in common with old Mrs Durant than with her own family.

At this point it seems strange that Louisa's attitude should be characterised as 'stubborn', 'obstinate' and 'sulky'. Her appraisal of the Durants is more fair-minded than that of her parents, which she contests. The third section, however, shows that this fair-mindedness is fortuitous. Louisa will stick to her guns, whether or not she has reason on her side. It is Mr Massy who is the incarnation of 'pure justice'. Louisa's refusal to give him credit for it—her refusal to join in the general practice of suppressing hatred—is undoubtedly obstinate. Mary, of course, is anything but obstinate, and the implication of acknowledging 'mental' superiority is symbolised in her eventual subjection to Mr Massy. What she hoped to achieve by marrying him was to 'get rid of her body'. As has already been shown, however, this is impossible, witness the large family automatically produced by Mr Lindley, and more generally the repeated suggestion that subjection to mental coercion produces malignant inner growths. Mrs Lindley swells with suppressed hatred; Mr Lindley is taken seriously ill; M

Massy has 'an internal trouble'; Mrs Durant's 'complaint' at last ceases to be merely vocal and becomes a tumour. This is the fate from which Louisa obstinately seeks to break free, the fate of Mary who comes to realise that through her marriage she is 'murdering herself' (a fair translation of *self-sacrifice*). Although unreasonable, therefore, Louisa's contempt for Mr Massy is healthy.

Dealing as we are, from this point onwards, with dark forces that take over from reason, especially when so many people think they know what Lawrence believed about such matters, it is important to note that these irrational forces are not morally blind. Louisa's irrational disgust for Mr Massy crystallises at the bedside of the dying Mr Durant. In the contrast presented between the clergyman's repulsive figure and the glowing health of the young sailor, Mr Massy's deficiency is, admittedly, portrayed as physical, but a moral deficiency is also presented, for example in his characteristic enquiry about the dying man: 'Has he any understanding?' Mr Massy does his duty at the bedside, but although he does the right thing, everything he does is wrong when it is viewed through the sympathetic eye which perceives Mrs Durant's need to give in and cling to her son. Sympathising with Mrs Durant, and therefore with Louisa, the reader recognises the difference between two kinds of human relationship—the one formal, and socially guaranteed, the other spontaneous and hazardous. A formal relationship calls for the eradication of spontaneous responses between individuals, a suppression of vitality which Louisa is not prepared to make. Spontaneous relationship thrives on natural responses, but requires an exposure to pain which Mr Massy, like all the other characters who live inside shells, is afraid of.

By the end of the third section a moral framework has thus been solidly erected. It consistently enriches and is enriched by the ensuing story of Mr Massy and Mary. This consistency is too detailed to be traced in full, either here or in the classroom. In the classroom it is sufficient to develop those points where it is particularly felt by individual readers. There is, however, more than consistency. Once again there is extension, as the story grows. The fact that physical life cannot be eliminated, but only perverted, receives its fullest manifestation in the revelation of Mr Massy's character. That he is less than human has already been indicated by repeated mention of the way in which he 'pads' rather than walks. His stunted body now turns out to be the outward sign of the retardation, not the eradication, of his impulses. These differ from those of other men only in their blind insensitivity and egoism. So, when Mary accepts his proposal of marriage, she feels 'the male in him, something cold and triumphant, asserting itself'; he is engrossed by the baby's needs, but never plays with it; as Louisa had intuitively perceived, the exclusive cultivation of his mind had not made him an angel—'scrupulously just and kind' although he might be—but an 'imbecile'.

Mary, on the other hand, extends the pattern in the opposite direction, that of the admiration shown from the beginning for the heroism of those who subject themselves to an ideal. 'She had sold a lower thing, her body, for a higher thing, her freedom from material things. . . . There remained only the direction of her activity towards charity and high-minded living.' Her loyalty to this bargain, despite her discovery that 'there was something in the bargain she had not understood', her inability to remain cold to her children, her dignified refusal to dissociate herself from her humiliating husband, and her lonely attempt to be fair to Alfred Durant, all combine with the queenly atmosphere with which Lawrence surrounds her to give her tragic stature. It is impossible to feel for her the contempt inspired by Mr Lindley, much less the revulsion inspired by Mr Massy, although she stands on the same side of the fence with them, *if* a fence is to be erected. But the story does not erect fences. To herd its characters into classified pens would be to do it the same kind of vital injury which so many of them, in the narrative, inflict upon themselves.

Yet Mary has done something wrong, which estranges her from Louisa. Indeed, she has done even more wrong than Louisa can perceive, because her marriage involves her in a false relationship to her husband, viewed from the standpoint of a personal, as opposed to an impersonal, morality. It is a defensive transaction, not a living response. 'Rigorously she kept to her position. She took care of him and was just to him.' She offers him not herself but only his marital rights (just as she argues merely for the rights of Alfred and Louisa at the end of the story). The satisfaction of this 'position' is the emotional 'independence' it secures. If you voluntarily deny your feeling, to offer people their rights, you escape the risk of involuntarily offering them something more, and obviously they have no *right* to ask for more.

This 'position' is mirrored in Alfred's relationship with his mother. When we first see him comforting her at his father's bedside, he presents a picture of natural feeling for Louisa to contrast with Mr Massy's personification of punctilious duty, but this is because their habitual form of life has been temporarily broken by shock. As Louisa comes to realise, they are not accustomed to spontaneous exchanges. They do their 'duty' by each other, render each other 'services', and respect each others' 'rights'. (These are key-words throughout the story, but especially in this part of it. Even when she protests at Louisa's kindness, Mrs Durant says, 'I'm sure you've no right to trouble yourself.') The old woman has done her duty by her children, but the only part of it she enjoyed has been running the shop. The rest is bitterness and futility, for reasons which become dramatically apparent in her sudden fatal illness. She and Alfred are separated from each other. Their deep feelings remain underground, because they cling to their habitual relationship which has always been defensively formal. Even at this moment, her only apparent concern for him is 'a cruel attention to his needs', while he can only take his lead from her.

Daughters of the Vicar

'How do you feel?' he said to his mother.

'It's a bit better,' she replied, wearily, impersonally. This strange putting aside herself, this abstracting herself and answering him only what she thought good for him to hear, made the relations between mother and son poignant and cramping to Miss Louisa. It made the man so ineffectual, so nothing.

Alfred's ineffectuality is very similar to that of Mr Lindley. 'Out of humiliation and self-hatred' he has risen to 'a sort of inner freedom'. But Alfred is not set in this position. He suffers under the 'secret burden of his unknown, unbestowed self', and can be shocked out of his shell. The shock of seeing Louisa in his mother's bedroom in the morning gives his imprisoned self strength. 'He stood almost himself, determined.' But, after all, instead of exposing himself by telling his mother that he will not go to work that day, whatever she says, because she needs him, he dutifully accepts her dutiful direction to go to the mine as usual. (Mr Massy, one recalls, was also 'unself-ish'.)

The self which Alfred's mind denies expresses itself in his body. As an emotion, he is almost unconscious of his grief at his mother's illness, but it makes itself felt as a physical pain which 'had nothing to do with his thoughts'. When he finally breaks his shell, yielding to his need for Louisa, this hatching of his unknown self is accompanied by convulsive movements. This stress on the physical is in place and convincing, as is also the way in which Louisa comes to 'see' him personally, as she has previously only 'seen' her sister, through touching his body when she washes his back.

'How funny he looks with his face upside down,' she thought. After all, there was a difference between her and the common people. The water in which his arms were plunged was quite black, the soap-froth was darkish. She could scarcely conceive him as human. Mechanically, under the influence of habit, he groped in the black water, fished out soap and flannel, and handed them backward to Louisa. Then he remained rigid and submissive, his two arms thrust straight in the panchion, supporting the weight of his shoulders. His skin was beautifully white and unblemished, of an opaque, solid whiteness. Gradually Louisa saw it: this also was what he was. It fascinated her. Her feelings of separateness passed away: she ceased to draw back from contact with him and his mother. There was this living centre. Her heart ran hot. She had reached some goal in this beautiful, clean, male body. She loved him in a white, impersonal heat. But the sun-burnt, reddish neck and ears: they were more personal, more curious. A tenderness rose in her, she loved even his queer ears. A person, an intimate being he was to her.

This scene proceeds through stages of personal awareness in which the purely physical plays an essential part, but it is impossible to read it as an account of a conventional relationship being superseded by a sexual one. Lawrence prevents this by the care with which he registers the changes from a defensive, formal awareness, to a passive, physical one, and from that onward to a positively personal one. But the writing is not couched in doctrinal terms. We see Louisa as she sees Alfred. At the beginning of the passage she forces her response with the familiar Lindley mould. She sees him merely as a member of another class. Then the impersonal impact of the body as a living thing—not as a 'form of life'—overwhelms this defence mechanism. Following this, however, personal recognition dawns. 'A tenderness rose in her, she loved even his queer ears.' This, we know, is what she has been waiting for—in the profound sense, because her refusal to deny her hate (being simply a refusal to deny her deepest feelings) was made so that she might love, and, in the narrative sense, because from hints and signs starting with the early luncheon scene, we have seen her falling in love with Alfred. Of course, this does not mean that their relationship is now secure, or even that her love is. He has only to put his clothes on for her to feel a stranger, and the certainty of the formal relationship tempts her. 'Oh, if she could only find some fixed relations, something sure and abiding.' But we know that, after what has happened, this relationship can never be fossilised.

By comparison with her relationship with him, or of his with his mother, and (on their rare encounters) with the rest of the Lindley family, Alfred's relationship with Louisa is forced. There is, perhaps, a schematic element in the way in which he is made to conform generally with the moral pattern of the story. It seems gratuitous, for example, to endow him with 'fixed ideas which he had got from the Fabians', neatly though this detail fits into the general framework. Certainly, the way in which he extends this framework into the erotic sphere is formulated instead of being presented. Passing reference to failures in brothels does not make his sexual alienation come to life as his filial alienation comes to life in his dealings with his mother. We are shown too little, and told too much. 'There were two things for him, the *idea* of women, with which he sometimes debauched himself, and real women, before whom he felt a deep uneasiness, and a need to draw away.'

Both Louisa and Lawrence demand that Alfred should love her, but the reader still has to be convinced. We can readily believe that Louisa rages at the way in which he holds her at a distance by treating her formally, and tells herself that it is 'cowardice', but we do not have to agree with her. When he treats his mother in this way, we can see that his behaviour is indeed cowardly, because he is evading something. But, unless we believe that formal relations are invariably a sign of the evasion of deep feeling, we have to be shown the deep feeling for Louisa which he is denying before we can see anything wrong in his politeness to her. 'She could see he felt real joy in doing anything for her, but any recognition would confuse him and hurt him.' Remembering the trenchancy of Louisa's recognitions, with which party are we to sympathise?

In the earlier part of the story he shows no interest in Louisa comparable with the interest she shows in him, and his vision of her, in the revelation scene in the cottage when his mother is dying, differs markedly from hers of him. It is not physical, but 'ideal' in exactly the way his vision of women in general has been described as being.

> As she sat writing, he placed another candle near her. The rather dense light fell in two places on the over-foldings of her hair till it glistened heavy and bright, like a dense golden plumage folded up. Then the nape of her neck was very white, with fine down and pointed wisps of gold. He watched it as if it were a vision, losing himself. She was all that was beyond him, of revelation and exquisiteness. All that was ideal and beyond him, she was that—and he was lost to himself in looking at her.

This, surely, is infatuation, not love. He does not 'see' her hair in the way she saw his ears. When she finally asks him, 'Don't you want me?', therefore, the true answer, as far as we know, should have been, 'Not really.'

Once this corner has been turned, however, nothing could be more convincing than the sudden dissipation of tension, and establishment of normality—not ordinariness, which is what formality would reduce life to, but normality—of their intimacy.

> 'Your face is black,' she said.
> He laughed.
> 'Yours is a bit smudged,' he said.
> They were afraid of each other, afraid to talk. He could only keep her near to him. After a while she wanted to wash her face. He brought her some warm water, standing by and watching her. There was something he wanted to say, that he dared not. He watched her wiping her face, and making tidy her hair.
> 'They'll see your blouse is dirty,' he said.
> She looked at her sleeves and laughed for joy.

Against this sanity, the unhealthy and uncomfortable family pressures exercised by the Lindley family, although painful, are completely powerless. The formality of the interview with Mr Lindley shows what a feeble thing, in the end, formality is.

We have suggested a final appraisal of the story through the comparison of analogous scenes: the teacher might, for example, invite comparison of Mr Massy's request to Mr Lindley for his daughter's hand with Alfred's, or of the two scenes in which the two men declare themselves as lovers. Our other suggestion was close examination of a passage to determine why it contains the particular words it does. The passages which lend themselves most easily to this treatment are those where the vocabulary has a moral force: the opening section, on re-reading, yields many sentences which reward careful examination, as, for example, the statement that Mr Lindley lacked 'the strength to impose himself where he would have liked to be recognised' which gains much in the context of Louisa's story. A very special interest, however, attaches to those passages where the significance of detail is metaphorical, because they show the Shakespearian quality of the imagination at work. An instance in point is the opening of Section X, describing Alfred's return to the cottage on the evening his mother is taken ill.

> By the big gate of the railway, in the fence, was a little gate that he kept locked. As he unfastened it he watched the kitchen light that shone on to the bushes and the snow outside. It was a candle burning till night set in, he thought to himself. He slid down the steep path to the level below. He liked making the first marks in the smooth snow. Then he came through the bushes to the house.

The preceding sections have analysed Alfred's psychological state and described him coming up from the pit. The immediately ensuing sections are to narrate the decisive irruption of Louisa into his life. In this context it is not difficult to see, in the detail of the little locked gate in the fence, a metaphor for the condition of his imprisoned self. The image of the little light surrounded by a threatening darkness similarly suggests the alienation of his conscious self from the forces it holds at bay.

The latter implication has already been established in the preceding section, where, as soon as he has arrived by the pit cage in 'the upper world', there is a sustained contrast of small lights against a surrounding darkness, reinforced by a similar contrast between the purity of freshly fallen snow and its subsequent defilement by contact with human activity. In that passage, however, Alfred feels sympathy for the virgin snow. In this passage he enjoys acting on it. (The reader familiar with Lawrence's work will at once recall the famous 'Moony' chapter, where Birkin shatters the moon's reflection in a pond.) There is therefore a tension in the symbolism, expressive of the tension in Alfred's inner life. Despite his locked inner gate, he enjoys sliding 'down the steep path to the level below'. Compare, on the previous page, his reaction to the descent of tufts of snow down the mine shaft into the pit: 'He wondered how it liked its excursion underground.'

And the image of the burning candle shares in this ambiguity. It is not only an image of separation. The image of Louisa now to be presented is a persistently glowing one, and this same candle will play its part both in the scene (already quoted) where he gazes at her hair, and the scene next morning, when lifting his hand from the candle he suddenly sees her in bed beside his mother.

11

ON BEING 'WITH IT'

'WITH it' is the sort of slang often on the lips of the English teacher who seeks to demonstrate that in his case at least the 'generation gap' does not exist. Out of deference to the sensibilities of such a teacher we have omitted all reference to Captain Marryat's excellent *The Children of the New Forest*. We could not, however, avoid consideration of *Treasure Island*, and at this stage we imagine him protesting that although we began promisingly enough with Michael Bond, Meindert DeJong and Rosemary Sutcliff, as our pupils have advanced to maturity we have regressed into the nineteenth century. 'What about Stan Barstow, Alan Sillitoe, Keith Waterhouse, or John Braine?' he may ask. We even have the curious impression that he might add William Golding to this list. But how this list dates him!

The usual assumption behind the publication of school editions of such books as *Billy Liar* is that they handle contemporary issues which *directly* engage the interest of a teenager. There are two objections to this: (1) Is it a good thing to encourage identification with fictitious characters? As we have seen even in the cases of Jim Hawkins and Huckleberry Finn, the result of a sensitive reading is sympathy rather than identification: and we all know what a menace Hamlet has been to young men. (2) In current discussion characters like Arthur Seaton have been transformed into stereotypes (for which the authors are not to blame) and identification with a sterotype is the last thing one hopes will result from the teaching of English.

In any case are these heroes really more like us than are the heroes of the past? In fact few industrial workers find much resemblance between themselves and Arthur Seaton if the reactions of apprentices are anything to go by. Already the very characteristics which made him the representative topical subject of a BBC programme in 1961 serve now to render him a period piece, whereas Long John Silver continues to interest. He is the product of art as opposed to documentary. Merely 'contemporary' heroes date at the same pace as the teacher.

If the issues raised by works of art are the burning questions of their day, publicly debated, this is mere coincidence. We do not read *Felix Holt* for its politics, or *Tess of the d'Urbervilles* for its opinions on the plight of unmarried mothers. In the first place, works of art easily advert us to the social and moral framework of their day, insofar as these are relevant, and often down to the finest detail; and in the second place the questions which they open are usually regarded as closed both when they were written and today. This is because they are major questions—love, marriage, friendship, allegiance, parenthood, etc.—which no society is happy to have challenged at any but a superficial level.

Of course there are contemporary novelists who raise these questions in a way particularly interesting because it *is* contemporary. But the teacher need not add to his duties those of the pioneering literary critic in an uncharted world. It is his task to equip his pupils to read them for themselves, when they leave school or enter the sixth form. To equip in this sense does not, of course, mean to train in the application of a set procedure involving the deployment of such concepts as character, plot, and theme. It means rather to alert the pupil to a full sense of implication. That is to say, to encourage him to trust his own complete response even when he is initially tempted to feel that the author is trying to evoke a different response. If his suspicion about the author is justified he will have been, for the moment at least, a literary critic. If, on the other hand, his suspicions are not justified his experience of the book will have been more complete. Thus a boy reading *Treasure Island* with the belief that he is obliged to regard Dr Livesey as an irreproachable character will recoil from the work. But if he gives full play to his antipathies he will be rewarded. He will find that Stevenson has been beforehand.

As a final demonstration of the uses of this kind of alertness we shall now consider three very different short works by major authors which are particularly suited, because of their brevity, to the kind of sixth-form study which ought to run parallel to preparation for examinations. These are *Daisy Miller*, *The Dead*, and *Un Cœur Simple*.

Daisy Miller

The odd thing about Henry James's most popular novella is that it, like *Pride and Prejudice*, like *Huckleberry Finn*, and like D. H. Lawrence's *Daughters of the Vicar*, concerns codes of behaviour—their clash and their effect on what the reader feels to be genuine 'life'. Perhaps this is a fact about the novel in general. But it seems odd in James because his tone and setting are so radically different from those of Twain and Lawrence. A first impression will be very much that of a period piece: a perfect little story about the leisured international society of the late Victorian era, told in an urbane, almost bantering manner, and avoiding direct involvement with any but the lighter sides of life (and death).

Well, it would be an exaggeration to call Daisy a tragic heroine. Nevertheless we feel that it is both true *and* recognisable by a sixth-form class that James is, however urbanely, confronting some very important issues. And, oddly again, that some of these issues—the important ones—are extremely up-to-date: for Daisy is after all, socially if not sexually, the brave little advocate of 'doing your own thing'—material for all our own chatter, as well as that of an expatriate Roman society in which it was absurdly easy to distinguish between a gentleman and various forms of imitation (Eugenio, Giovanelli), about 'permissiveness'.

This point can only be well taken by those who have developed, or are being taught to develop, *critical* powers. Powers which will, in this case, enable them to distinguish the author's point of view from that of the ostensible hero, Winterbourne. James is so finished and clearly dexterous a writer that we seem smoothly encouraged to take 'our young man' at his own valuation: a skilled connoisseur of life and people, the true appreciator of Daisy's qualities. Hence the muddle at the end. But surface charm should not have deceived us. For the whole point of the tale is that Winterbourne is not so heroic (or, perhaps, so 'gallant') as he should be.

He is obviously not a villain. But he behaves villainously to Daisy because, sympathetic as he is, he cannot *quite* break through the codes which bind him. It is typical of James that we should feel for and with him in the process. But it is also typical that the process is fully indicated. How should these points be brought out in class reading? First we should consider what Winterbourne fails to see in Daisy, and the scene in the Pincian Gardens is obviously crucial to our understanding. Here James brings to bear on one another the full range of the codes he has already suggested. Mrs Walker is, at this point, a sympathetic personage, especially in contrast to the coldly snobbish Mrs Costello. She *is* trying to save Daisy from 'ruining' herself, if not from the fate worse than death. And it is clear that Daisy's response is silly and in a way ungrateful. Although we share her view that walking with a 'gentleman' in a public place is not a particularly ruinous activity, we can also see that it *is* so socially in the eyes of all the relevant spectators *and* that (as any post-pubescent girl who has visited Italy will be able to confirm) it does have real dangers. Daisy does not see, or will not acknowledge, either side of that code.

On Being 'With It'

Instead she insists on her own: 'I have never allowed a gentleman to dictate to me, or to interfere with anything I do' and (as the muted row with Mrs Walker gains in intensity): 'I don't think I want to know what you mean. . . . I don't think I should like it'. Here Daisy is not being simply foolish but morally assertive: she rejects all that the accepted code implies and insures against—that young girls cannot take care of themselves and will be seduced unless surrounded by a rigid hedge of decorum. And she does this with a naive delicacy. She is not an abandoned young person, but an idealist. However, like most idealists, she ends by going too far. She dies of a symbolic fever contracted by asserting herself too much in the old and unhealthy places.

Winterbourne's case is altogether different: and we would rest on it the conclusion that the story ultimately 'comes down' in favour of Daisy's crude innocence. Winterbourne (and the pupil will need little prompting to see the significance of his name) has nearly, but not quite, been codified out of existence. He is amazed by Daisy, and James gently makes his limitations clear from the very start. 'He had a great relish for feminine beauty; he was addicted to observing and analysing it; and as regards this young lady's face he made several observations.' The stilted air echoes the sterile response, and draws attention to the peculiarly detached vocabulary and the implicit metaphor of 'relish' (Gentleman's Relish?).

> Was she simply a pretty girl from New York State—were they all like that, the pretty girls who had a good deal of gentlemen's society? Or was she also a designing, and audacious, an unscrupulous young person? Winterbourne had lost his instinct in this matter, and his reason could not help him . . . she was only a pretty American flirt. Winterbourne was almost grateful for having found the formula that applied to Miss Daisy Miller.

Consider the contrast between 'instinct' and 'formula'. Again 'Winterbourne was impatient to see her again, and he was vexed with himself that, by instinct, he should not appreciate her justly.' Is the irony here that he does appreciate her by instinct, but *not* when consciously applying his range of social codifications? And so on—the attentive reader will find many more hints leading up to Winterbourne's ultimate disastrous act of impercipience in the Colosseum—there, at last, he *has* placed her!—and to the rebuke near the 'raw protuberance among the April daisies' in the Protestant Cemetery which is given by the guilty and humble Giovanelli:

'At last he said, "She was the most beautiful young lady I ever saw, and the most amiable." And then he added in a moment, "And she was the most innocent." ' It is not only the innocence that Winterbourne has failed to perceive, but also the beauty of one who he has insistently patronised as 'pretty'.

As we have said: all these are considerations concerning the way in which a hero fails to be heroic, and thus are about authorial distance and distancing. They should therefore reinforce the lessons learnt about reading from *Great Expectations*.

As usual much else could be suggested to a class. For example the following conversation between Winterbourne and Mrs Costello could be examined as a dramatic statement of the theme:

'They are very dreadful people.'
Winterbourne meditated a moment. 'They are very ignorant—very innocent only. Depend upon it they are not bad.'
'They are hopelessly vulgar,' said Mrs Costello. 'Whether or no being hopelessly vulgar is being "bad" is a question for the metaphysicians. They are bad enough to dislike, at any rate; and for this short life that is quite enough.'

On Being 'With It'

Or, if some pupils are likely to have a further interest in clichés about Henry James, some discussion of how the story fits in with the common idea that 'America' for him represented fresh spontaneity and 'Europe' a rich, hierarchical, codified corruption, could be initiated—clearly these ideas are too simple: how? Or lastly, and in a related discussion, some analysis of why we find such interchanges as the following funny in an especially Jamesian manner might be done:

> 'My father's name is Ezra B. Miller,' he announced. 'My father ain't in Europe; my father's in a better place than Europe.'
>
> Winterbourne imagined for a moment that this was the manner in which the child had been taught to intimate that Mr Miller had been removed to the sphere of celestial rewards. But Randolph immediately added, 'My father's in Schenectady. He's got a big business. My father's rich, you bet.'
>
> 'Well!' ejaculated Miss Miller. . . .

All this, of course, depends on the pupil's confidence in his own initial judgement of Winterbourne. Without that he would have accepted all the latter's opinions at face value and thus missed the point of the story.

The Dead

The case is very different with James Joyce. Although a responsive reading is essential, it is only to a further, reconsidered, almost speculative reading that *The Dead* reveals its full implication. The first reading in no way approximates to, or even resembles, a final one. It is only a preliminary exercise, ending in a scene which serves as a sign-post to send the reader back to the beginning with an eye alerted to features quite different from those which engaged his interest at first.

Teaching Fiction in Schools

What first engages interest is the story's realism. Joyce, it seems, is so careful to get everything exactly right: the detailed inventory of the dishes served for dinner is an obvious example, but more distinctive and pervasive is the consistent deployment of characteristic clichés, which even the narrative prose itself sometimes adopts to set the tone, as in the opening sentence—'Lily, the caretaker's daughter, was literally run off her feet.' Such features will lead the teacher to a consideration of the question of 'style', but even more worthy of attention is the use of cliché in dialogue.

'I'd like nothing better this minute,' said Mr Browne stoutly, 'than a rattling fine walk in the country or a fast drive with a spanking good goer between the shafts.'
'We used to have a very good horse and trap at home,' said Aunt Julia, sadly.
'The never-to-be-forgotten Johnny,' said Mary Jane, laughing.

'Very like himself Mr X looks' an Irish acquaintance once observed, and very like themselves Mr Browne, Aunt Julia and Mary Jane sound in this passage. In fact, it is more like mockery than reportage. But there is no derision in it. Joyce's irony is always charitable. In the immediately ensuing scene, Gabriel, tramping round the hall in his galoshes, impersonates the horse that was so accustomed to working a mill that, driven into Dublin in style one day, it persisted in circling the statue of William III. Very like this horse is Gabriel, we can see, but the perception is not tinged with contempt. Coming towards the end of the story, however, this incident is part of a realisation, dawning on the reader, that there is more in all this than meets the eye. There is, for example, an odd sort of irony in the realism—an irony which exposes the limits of realism. Life-likeness is not a quality of life itself: the difference is cruelly illustrated when Aunt Julia sings 'Arrayed for the Bridal' (even if we ignore the pun). The life-likeness of the characters is thus, in one sense, bogus. It makes them doll-like to the point of rigor mortis, as the title *The Dead* indicates. For all that, however, they are none the less like many people still alive and kicking above ground.

Much of this can perhaps be expressed more simply by saying that the characters are fossilised types, but there are things about them which can never be said about fossils, as, for example, that they provoke affection, and, more importantly, that there is still a kind of hope for them, because their behaviour is not predictable. Why does Miss Ivors depart in that odd manner? Why is Mr D'Arcy, immediately after singing, so irritated? It might be argued that these two characters are distinctively adventurous. Miss Ivors' message is 'Go West' (and at this stage, we do not register its ambiguity). Mr D'Arcy prefers the present to the past. But how about Freddy Malins? He turns up, exactly as expected, the worse for drink and behaving like a zombie. (Note the automatically repeated movement of rubbing his left fist into his left eye.) As the evening progresses, however, he goes on to display surprising but continuing courtesy, solicitude, and liberality of mind. We start with him being entrusted to the custody of Mr Browne, but end with Gabriel remarking: 'It's a pity he wouldn't keep away from that Browne, because he's not a bad fellow really.' He certainly remains a type, and yet—to anticipate our attention to symbols—his goose is not yet cooked. He makes the point himself, in the incident that follows his earnest compliments to Aunt Julia on her singing.

> Aunt Julia smiled broadly and murmured something about compliments as she released her hand from his grasp. Mr Browne extended his open hand towards her and said to those who were near him in the manner of a showman introducing a prodigy to an audience:
> 'Miss Julia Morkan, my latest discovery!'
> He was laughing at this very heartily himself when Freddy Malins turned to him and said:

'Well, Browne, if you're serious you might make a worse discovery....'

The point, made on behalf of all the 'dead', is 'never say die' (or 'Hinnegan').

The great discovery, of course, is the discovery of Gabriel. Even when the story is almost ended, when he and Gretta have arrived at last alone together in the hotel, nothing could seem further from the truth than her wifely tribute: 'You are a very generous person, Gabriel.' And yet, in the end, we are to be convinced that this is indeed so, by his acknowledgement of Michael Furey's superiority. 'Generous tears filled Gabriel's eyes. He had never felt like that himself towards any woman, but he knew that such a feeling must be love.' This generosity springs from humility, the humility of self-knowledge he has been staving off all evening, from the moment Lily, in answer to his condescending question about her 'young man', bursts out: 'The men that is now is only all palaver and what they can get out of you.' From that point we watch him trying to preserve his sense of superiority. The 'deadness' of those around him is all too plain to him and he desperately refuses to acknowledge that he belongs among them until comparison with Michael Furey, the man who really did belong in heroic cold, outside their smug world, compels him to see himself.

> He saw himself as a ludicrous figure, acting as a pennyboy for his aunts, a nervous, well-meaning sentimentalist, orating to vulgarians and idealising his own clownish lusts, the pitiable fellow he had caught a glimpse of in the mirror. Instinctively he turned his back more to the light....

To the defects he lists needs only be added the petty selfishness, manifest, for example, in his response to Gretta's wish to go to Galway—'You can go if you like'—and in his plan to get his own back on Miss Ivors, in his speech.

On Being 'With It'

An idea came into his mind and gave him courage. He would say, alluding to Aunt Kate and Aunt Julia: 'Ladies and Gentlemen, the generation which is now on the wane among us may have had its faults, but for my part I think it had certain qualities of hospitality, of humour, of humanity, which the new and very serious and hyper-educated generation that is growing up around us seems to me to lack.' Very good: that was one for Miss Ivors. What did he care that his aunts were only two ignorant old women?

At the end, instead of this callousness, we have his feelings of 'friendly pity', another term for the charity which, as already noted, informs the whole work.

And this, it might well seem, is enough for any pupil, a humane and accurately observed rediscovery of the impulse upon which society, in its deepest sense, depends—and a rediscovery which he can make for himself. The teacher's help is rarely needed, once the pupil is aware of the peculiar form of irony (an irony which witholds judgement). One additional point on which help may however be needed is in establishing a distinction between Gabriel's discoveries and those of the reader. Gabriel is never more than a character, and the full weight of the story does not lie behind his personal acknowledgement of Michael Furey's superiority. 'Better pass boldly into that other world, in the full glory of some passion, than fade and wither dismally with age.' The goose, to mention it again, is of the same feather as Ibsen's *Wild Duck*. Cliché may not adequately express life lived to the full, but then, neither does suicide.

As the final scene nears its end, however, a process develops, marked by an increasing solemnity of style, whereby Gabriel's vision becomes increasingly impersonal. This culminates in the celebrated last paragraph, describing the snow that falls not just in Dublin but generally, all over Ireland, indeed throughout the universe 'like the descent of their last end, upon all the living and the dead'. The concluding explicit comparison insists upon the metaphorical force of the entire description, and despite its highly-wrought quality—its obtrusive repetitions, alliterations and inversions—the image is a powerful one. We may place the phrase, 'his soul swooned slowly', as ironically as we place phrases from Gabriel's speech, such as 'living in a less spacious age'— in a way, that is, which Joyce does not intend. Nevertheless, the word 'swooned' is exact. There is something yielding, a feminine element of surrender, in Gabriel's response to this visible rendering of the normally imperceptible trend of human life. An illuminating comparison can be made with a metaphor of George Eliot's (from *Middlemarch*)—'the roar on the farther side of silence'. Both images render perceptible a gradual process by speeding it up. George Eliot's image, however, communicates an urgent need to make a moral effort before it is too late. The process made perceptible in Joyce's image, on the other hand, is inevitable. To make another comparison, however, although the process it pictures is one of obliteration, it does not communicate a sense of life as an insubstantial pageant, as does Wallace Stevens' image of the impermanence of human life compared with the permanence of rock. Stevens' image leads to reflection like:

> .... It is not to be believed.
> The meeting at noon at the edge of the field seems like
> An invention, an embrace between one desperate clod
> And another in a fantastic consciousness,
> In a queer assertion of humanity:

The objects heaped with snow in Joyce's image are too solid for that. We are not left with any sense that there is something queer about the assertion of humanity, by phrases like—'the lonely churchyard on the hill where Michael Furey lay buried'. As we suggested at the start, if his response to this vision now returns the reader to the foregoing story, expecting to perceive beneath its realistic surface the operation of ultimate forces, he will not be disappointed. The realistic details are also symbolic, and operate on two levels at once. A pupil who has read D. H. Lawrence's *Daughters of the Vicar* in depth will be well prepared for this development. He will not, of course, be prepared to follow up all the clues which the ingenious Joyce has planted in the story. The bulk of these we shall accordingly ignore, attending only to those which the genius Joyce, whether from natural growth or from grafting, brings to such fruition that, upon re-reading, even before we can identify it we feel that there is something extra there. The difference between these two kinds of devices is that those which are merely ingenious—the significance of personal names, for example—depend upon erudite reference to matters external to the story, while the compelling ones derive their force from features of the narrative with which they are significantly associated.

An example of the latter process is provided by the two pictures in the drawing room. What is the point of mentioning that one represents the balcony scene in *Romeo & Juliet*, the other the murdered Princes in the Tower? Probably an answer will not be immediately forthcoming. The pupil, re-reading, can wait until he returns to the crucial scene where Gabriel, at the foot of the stairs, looks up at his wife as she leans on the bannister near the top, listening to Mr D'Arcy's song. He may then notice the words of that song—'My babe lies cold.' Another tracer, similarly conveying a sense of fatality which is wholly appropriate, is the image of fingering a glass which separates two worlds. Thus, when he wishes he was alone outside in the snow, 'Gabriel's warm, trembling fingers tapped the cold pane of the window.' At the end of the final paragraph, the situation is reversed. The snow summons Gabriel. 'A few light taps upon the pane made him turn to the window.' In this case, however, a full appreciation of the significance of the coincidence depends upon a sense of what the snow means. It is, of course, as we have seen, an image of obliteration, but it is also more than that. It is a source of beauty, alike transforming the Wellington Monument and the statue of Daniel O'Connell, 'the Liberator', with an impartiality like that of the proverbial rain. It is the embodiment of a light, luminous, white cold, simplifying force which operates against a heavy, glowing, brown, warm, harmonious one.

Note how, in the fatal moment when Gretta hears the song, this force intensifies her costume by cancellation. As Gabriel gazed, 'he could see the terra-cotta and salmon-pink panels of her skirt which the shadow made appear black and white'. It might well alarm the teacher to hear a pupil say that the whole movement of the story is implicit in that sentence, but a sensitive reading of the story guided by a sense of the polarities indicated should at least convince that, as it progresses, it accumulates additional meaning exactly along these lines.

Although Gabriel is afraid of real snow from the beginning, and unlike Gretta prudently protects himself from it in galoshes, it is only at the end that he sees it for what it is. Once he is safe inside his aunts' house he idealises the snow outside, as representing a freedom from the convention and domestic falsity with which he refuses to associate himself. Even when he stands up to make his pompous speech, he is aware of it in this way.

> Gabriel leaned his ten trembling fingers on the table cloth and smiled nervously at the company. Meeting a row of upturned faces he raised his eyes to the chandelier. The piano was playing a waltz tune and he could hear the skirts sweeping against the drawing-room door. People, perhaps, were standing in the snow on the quay outside, gazing up at the lighted windows and listening to the waltz music. The air was pure there. In the distance lay the park, where the trees were weighted with snow. The Wellington Monument wore a gleaming cap of snow that flashed westward over the white fields of Fifteen Acres.

On Being 'With It'

The reader will recognise in this passage the presence not only of the snow, but also other elements of the clusters we have sketched. Thus light, too, is an element of the picture of escape—even in the chandelier. As for the music, it is worth remembering that Gabriel did not enjoy it that evening.

He also endows his idealised, as opposed to his actual, relationship with Gretta with similar elements of luminosity. Light features prominently in each of his uxorious glimpses of her. The same is true of lightness. She appears almost like a snow-flake in passages of sentimental release, such as the following.

> She was walking on before him so lightly and so erect that he longed to run after her noiselessly, catch her by the shoulders and say something foolish and affectionate into her ear. She seemed to him so frail that he longed to defend her against something and then to be alone with her. Moments of their secret life together burst like stars upon his memory.

The falsity of his mood, expressed in moral terms, is that it ignores the starkness inherent in the kind of freedom he claims as his right to distinction. Expressed in simple physical terms, the falsity lies in overlooking the fact, tacitly acknowledged by his galoshes, that snow is cold. But it is to escape a cold journey that he has taken a hotel room for the night, and, in the end, the image of Michael Furey freezing to death compels him to see snow for what it is.

The opposing cluster of what might be called mahogany images is largely confined to indoors, though it extends into the city as the thaw exposes it to view.

> A dull yellow light brooded over the houses and the river; and the sky seemed to be descending. It was slushy underfoot, and only streaks and patches of snow lay on the roofs, on the parapets of the quay and on the area

railings. The lamps were still burning redly in the murky air and, across the river, the palace of the Four Courts stood out menacingly against the heavy sky.

A pretty example of the consistency with which this pattern is employed is afforded by the ensuing description of Gretta walking through the slushy street. She 'no longer had any grace of attitude', and was accordingly carrying a brown paper parcel. Only a reader with Joyce's superstitious passion for words will, however, appreciate the accident of the name of the sociable Mr Browne (who, as Aunt Kate remarks, is everywhere), or the intrusion of references to Browning.

The warm, brown element becomes increasingly dominant in the story, from the moment Gretta and Gabriel enter from the snowy street, and although it cannot triumph in the end it enjoys its moment of triumph in the festal consumption of the fat brown goose—a fitting emblem of its victory over the cold, white element. It is not just that geese are white. Their connection with snow is proverbial, and so too, at least in Ireland, their connection with untamed freedom. Gabriel, who likes to consider himself a free spirit, treads, or rather cycles, ignominiously in the footsteps of 'the wild geese' every summer, when he goes on a continental holiday 'with some fellows'. His proper relationship with wild flight, however, is demonstrated when he carves the goose and offers somebody a wing. That this tameness has a positive value becomes evident, despite all the sentimentality and indignity, as his cliché-laden speech comes to an end, and he gives the toast. Although we have noticed how, as he ceased speaking, 'every member of the company fingered a glass expectantly' (sic!), they are not just enjoying a drink in the action that ensues. Although it is written in a dexterously secondhand style (which surprisingly reveals Freddy Malins to be a close relation of the Cratchits), this description is more convincing than the final paragraph about the snow because it is not overdone.

On Being 'With It'

All the guests stood up, glass in hand, and turning towards the three ladies, sang in unison, with Mr Browne as leader:

'For they are jolly gay fellows,
For they are jolly gay fellows,
For they are jolly gay fellows,
Which nobody can deny.'

Aunt Kate was making frank use of her handkerchief and even Aunt Julia seemed moved. Freddy Malins beat time with his pudding-fork and the singers turned towards one another, as if in melodious conference, while they sang with emphasis:

'Unless he tells a lie,
Unless he tells a lie.'

Then, turning once more towards their hostesses, they sang:

'For they are jolly gay fellows,
For they are jolly gay fellows,
For they are jolly gay fellows,
Which nobody can deny.'

The acclamation which followed was taken up beyond the door of the supper room by many of the other guests and renewed time after time, Freddy Malins acting as officer with his fork on high.

As Falstaff demonstrated at Shrewsbury, there are two kinds of dead.

At this point there is a break in the narrative, and when it is resumed the cold white element is claiming its turn, from the opening sentences.

The piercing morning air came into the hall where they were standing so that Aunt Kate said:

'Close the door, somebody. Mrs Malins will get her death of cold.'

Teaching Fiction in Schools

Is this, the student might be asked, all that the story has to offer—the realisation that you can't both keep your goose alive and eat it? Is it just a matter of seeing both sides? A different question should perhaps be considered first. What produces the two 'epiphanies', the apotheoses respectively of harmony and purity? The answer, surely, is that they both spring from unforced acts of homage to other people.

A Simple Heart

Such an act of homage—homage by a literary aristocrat to the plebeian and illiterate—is, we feel, the achievement of the last story we shall consider. We had intended to conclude this chapter with an account of a tale by Conrad. But 'Typhoon', 'The Secret Sharer', and 'The Shadow Line' are in a school's edition with an introduction by the late Douglas Brown which far excels anything we could provide; and *Heart of Darkness*, our other candidate, offers, besides an extraordinary complexity, an experience too strangely profound even for the sixth form. So why not step, at this late stage of school English, into foreign ground? It should not be the privilege of the bright and exploring pupil alone to discover the work of the European and Russian masters. They—Tolstoy, Turgenev, Chekhov, Stendhal, Balzac, etc., might even be systematically recommended to those with time to spend.

But of course, if we are expecting our pupils to be critics, the problem of translation has to be faced—or, rather, simply admitted to exist. The only mitigating factor is that it is prose fiction that is commonly held to lose least in translation. But even so we must be prepared always to step warily, and even to compare translations if opportunity and expertise are available or on loan. And this is particularly the case with the most notoriously deliberate of novelists, Flaubert. The justness of his words is very often likely to be lost—as in, for example, the grotesque play on the formal title 'Madame Bovary, Jeune' which is remorselessly used in referring to Charles Bovary's first, elderly, and decidedly scraggy, wife. Nevertheless it is to Flaubert that we intend to turn in recommending for attention a relatively easy work: the first of his *Three Tales (Trois Contes)*, 'A Simple Heart' ('Un Cœur Simple').

Here the utterly, even infuriatingly, flat and unemotional tone, the illusion of a dry and anonymous objectivity, does survive translation (at least that by Robert Baldick in the Penguin Classics). And the question it thus poses in an extreme form is an important one in the reading of all fiction. It takes Flaubert only forty pages to record a whole, and long, life. His art is obviously one of selection and compression, and his meaning to be found in the seemingly random incidents he chooses for representation rather than in any authorial commentary and analysis, or inclusion of a narrating *persona* (we hardly need to note that he had great influence on later writers, among them Conrad, Henry James, and Joyce, and that this influence is very largely of a 'technical' kind). But how then, especially since Félicité drags out so prosaic an existence, does the story avoid being a thorough bore? This is the key question.

Consider the following passage about Félicité's childhood, presented, typically, without comment:

> She went about in rags, shivering with cold, used to lie flat on the ground to drink water out of ponds, would be beaten for no reason at all, and was finally turned out of the house for stealing thirty sous, a theft of which she was innocent. She found work at another farm, looking after the poultry, and as she was liked by her employers the other servants were jealous of her.

Here we begin to appreciate the significance of the heroine's name. Flaubert slaps the world in the face and follows with a punch in the stomach without so much as the hint of a frown. It is all just fact, and the tone disallows any expression of surprise. The effect is therefore much more powerful than it would have been had Dickens been let loose on the subject of an off day. It is precisely the implication that this is *ordinary* behaviour that gives power.

Once this method—full of flat little sentences in flat little paragraphs—is grasped, we can begin to see something of Flaubert's purposes. We can also allow, as it were, the existence of detail which is strictly *irrelevant* but which gives the tale a curiously palpable life:

> As for the children, they were taught by Guyot, a poor devil employed at the Town Hall, who was famous for his beautiful handwriting, and who had a habit of sharpening his penknife on his boots.

This is the *mot* (i.e. perception) *juste* all right; but it has nothing of the precious literary dandyism usually associated with that phrase.

To return to Félicité's life as a reflection on mankind: it gradually becomes obvious that the simple heart is being used—not in a simple way for we remember her skill at haggling—to show—though not so violently as in *Madame Bovary*—the shabby selfishness which Flaubert saw as pervasive of his society. (Reflections on our own or other societies may be safely left to the pupil if he reads intelligently.) The following passage about the beloved Victor's death is merely one of many: it is quoted in preference to others because of its inclusiveness:

> Long afterwards she learnt the circumstances of Victor's death from the captain of his ship. He had gone down with yellow fever, and they had bled him too much at the hospital. Four doctors had held him at once. He had died straight away, and the chief doctor had said:
> 'Good! There goes another!'
> His parents had always treated him cruelly. She preferred not to see them again, and they made no advances, either because they had forgotten about her or out of the callousness of the poor.

On Being 'With It'

But then Victor wasn't much, was he? Flaubert writes here as the practical man, that is, the purveyor of facts and attitudes which are loathsome—but again, to make them more terrible, quite ordinary. He writes also as the author of the immediately preceding passage who knows through his creation of Félicité that his insights are, in a distinguished sense, commonplace:

> Mme Aubain was trembling slightly. She suggested that she [Félicité] should go and see her sister at Trouville, but Félicité shook her head to indicate that there was no need for that.
> There was a silence. Old Liébard thought it advisable to go.
> Then Félicité said:
> 'It doesn't matter a bit, not to them it doesn't.'
> Her head fell forward again, and from time to time she unconsciously picked up the knitting needles lying on the work-table.
> Some women went past carrying a tray full of dripping linen.
> Catching sight of them through the window, she remembered her own washing. . . .

We suggest that these features of the tale would be quite easy to point out in class reading. But are we, then, to accept them as the whole depressing burden of 'A Simple Heart'? Answers to this will, and have been, various. Nevertheless it seems to us that there was for Flaubert, and is, more in the tale than a clever rendering of nasty mediocrity. For Félicité, the reflector of mediocrity, is constantly present. It is her life we are concerned with. And it is no coincidence that, after the brief introductory section, it is announced that 'Like everyone else, she had had her love story.' A striking phrase, although consonant with the world-weary tone to which the reader is just accustoming himself. It turns out, of course, that the love story ends in brutal fiasco, and that

Teaching Fiction in Schools

our only further information about its hero sounds dubious and is drowned out by the noise of waggons and hooves. But it is nevertheless a clue to Flaubert's finer purpose—as much a clue as is, in retrospect, the title of the story (*cœur* having, if anything, stronger connotations in French than in English). Félicité is, in the starved conditions so ruthlessly exposed by the hater of the bourgeoisie, in search of love: for Théodore, for the (ironically named) Paul and Virginie, for Victor, for the soldiers, the Poles, and Père Colmiche, and finally for Loulou. Or rather, she is in search of something *to* love: and she finds it, of course, only in the parrot. That is why the tale is a tender grotesque rather than a tragedy or a piece of polished cynicism. As Peter de Vries says, 'What people believe is a measure of what they suffer.' But meanwhile, and before the famous and final apotheosis which shows that Félicité has in fact understood religion very well ('to minds like hers the supernatural is a simple matter'), the pupil might be asked what to make of the curious little scene after Virginie's death when she and Mme Aubain bring themselves to go through the relics of the dead:

> They found a little chestnut-coloured hat, made of plush with a long nap; but the moths had ruined it. Félicité asked if she might have it. The two women looked at each other and their eyes filled with tears. Then the mistress opened her arms, the maid threw herself into them, and they clasped each other in a warm embrace, satisfying their grief in a kiss which made them equal.
> It was the first time that such a thing had happened, for Mme Aubain was not of a demonstrative nature. Félicité was as grateful as if she had received a great favour, and henceforth loved her mistress with dog-like and religious veneration.
> Her heart grew softer as time went by.

This is a, if not the, climax of the work—and, despite the

On Being 'With It'

irony contained in the word 'equal', what a tremendous effect with materials so homely, related in so unemotional a manner! It would be an impercipient reader who could not see the significant connection of this with the very first paragraph: 'For half a century the women of Pont-l'Eveque envied Mme Aubain her maidservant Félicité....'

It would be tedious to elaborate such points. But we nevertheless contend that an intelligent reading of 'A Simple Heart' will expand the pupil's mind to the recognition both of the existence of a literature outside our own, and to yet another way—a particularly subtle way—in which an artist achieves his effects. Such an expansion could not take place if 'comprehension' alone were called for. And certainly a willed contemporaneity has nothing to do with it.

12

ENDS

OUR APPROACH to the teaching of literature in schools is, we hope, continuous with that advocated for the University by Dr F. R. Leavis in his very practical, but practically unheeded, *Education and the University* (1943), and reiterated with a further stress in response to a more desperate need in his recent *English Literature in our Time and the University*. It requires a teacher who himself as a reader possesses those qualities which he seeks to elicit in his pupils. There is no avoiding this awkward fact (although it may be some relief to Education Authorities to be informed of the fact—disquieting to others—that suitable teachers are hardly more likely to be found among graduates in English Literature, as the situation now is, than among any other body of educated men). Our approach *precludes* the complete integration of literature with other studies. Moreover, it entails that, unless every member of the 'team' was critically aware, literature could *not* be 'team-taught'. This, as we trust previous chapters have shown, is not to proclaim a new aestheticism. Nor is it to say that teachers of History or Geography who use extracts from *La Princesse de Clèves* or *Robinson Crusoe* to illuminate their themes are crudely trespassing. It is simply to assert that the unique value of literature can be discovered only through its unique disciplines. To adapt Dr Johnson: Literature 'must be seen before it can be known'. And teachers who *can* see, can impart their skills of vision, even to very young people.

There is a simple reason why so many English teachers are at present trying to find new ways of teaching literature. A revolution has been effected in English teaching by the realisation that lessons should, could, or might, take the form of a lively sharing of experience. We have commented on some aspects of this revolution in our first chapter. Paradoxically, however, literature—that promising source of liveliness and potency and precision in the language—has proved an awful disappointment. And to teachers and theorists who evidently are disappointed the solution seems increasingly to be to bring literature out of its own sufficiencies and into a close and improper embrace with what they call 'experience'. The odd thing is that while they can solemnly burn a piece of newspaper in the classroom in order to give their pupils a (gem-like?) experience to describe, they are unable to turn a novel to the same advantage. Novels of any length do not burn easily. But there *are* other things (such as we have suggested) to be done with them. They are perhaps not the sort of things which have been recommended to these teachers. Certainly the experience of reading a novel round the class, answering exhaustive and exhausting series of comprehension questions about it, and finally writing a letter (of at least two sides) recommending it to an unimaginable friend, is not a stimulant to self-expression. We sympathise with the teacher who boldly refuses to have much to do with literature if *this* is what teaching it means.

Our hope is that this book will have shown him that there is a third (literary) alternative to that current and alluring approach which, claiming that language governs all aspects of human activity, serves up as the version of an English lesson a hot-pot of Reality.

In this context all that we wish to assert (and it is a minimum) is that literature is real too—which is not to say that we wish to claim a place for it in the hot-pot. Nor do we

Teaching Fiction in Schools

wish to tip the hot-pot down the sink. English teaching, as John Dixon explains in *Growth through English* (1967), involves a comprehensive cluster of activities. Our point is that, however many these activities may be, the critical reading of imaginative literature is one of them, and must not be blended with the others. It is furthermore our belief that it should be the chief means and the great end of English study at any level. And it seems strange that in a climate which values 'awareness' so much, the most potently aware of human activities, literature, should be compounded with a mess of unorganised experience. We are well aware that our view is not universal among teachers. But, luckily, it is not necessary to share it in order to see the fallacies in the account of literature offered by John Dixon. *Growth through English* is the officially-sponsored report for specialists of the Conference on English Teaching, held at Dartmouth, New Hampshire, under the auspices of the Modern Language Association, and the National Council of Teachers of English (both of America), and the National Association for the Teaching of English (of Great Britain), financially supported by the Carnegie Foundation. It thus represents a not uninfluential body of pedagogic opinion. Its approach, which we may term 'global', is, as we have hinted, based on the theory that since language is the principal means whereby humanity structures Reality, English teaching is concerned with the apprehension of Reality in all its forms. And its naive objection to fiction as fiction is that it is not Reality. Criticising the effect upon teachers of the literary tradition, which he terms 'the heritage model' Mr Dixon states that it involves the teacher 'in presenting experience [in fictions] to his pupils, rather than drawing from them their experience [of reality and the self]'. The reader of the present book will, we hope, have realised that there is a third possibility, namely, that of 'drawing from' pupils their experience of fiction. Nevertheless it is worth examining the processes by which so many acute minds contrived to mislead one another at Dartmouth.

Ends

The basic error is the failure to recognise the fact that the word 'literature' implies a valuation. Not all fiction is literature in the eyes of cultivated persons. The Dartmouth Conference, however, sought to be scientific. It felt that English teaching could only rest safely and respectably on Linguistics and Sociology (poor old Civics!). Literature therefore was defined as a means of apprehending Reality, namely, a means whereby 'we experience life ... in the role of spectator and not participant'. 'During the Seminar', Mr Dixon reports, 'our sense of the role of spectator came to define the term "literature" in our discussions.' Through the wide eye of this needle any camel could pass: 'Though our central attention was for literature in the ordinary [sic!] sense we found it impossible to separate this sharply from the other stories, films, or TV plays, or from pupils' own personal writing or spoken narrative.'

The result of this extraordinary definition is disastrous for teaching literature in the 'ordinary sense'. Instead of directing his pupils' attention to the use of language, the teacher directs it into the street: 'if an interest in literature is to inform and modify our encounter with life itself, the teacher must bring into a vivid relationship life as it is enacted [i.e. fact] and life as it is represented [i.e. fiction]. For some of us this means a readiness to go outside the classroom walls, to meet people, observe them, and work with them, so that we and our pupils can draw from their experience and understanding.'

Mr Dixon's thought is governed by a series of stringent either/ors. As he sees it the only alternative to his method is 'looking at life through fictions' and taking no interest in Reality—which he categorises as a temptation. 'Those who succumb', he warns us, 'will dismiss as "sociology" an interest in the life of the city or the countryside.' While finding room to accommodate the interest in question along with our interest in literature, it is certainly as quasi-sociology that we dismiss his view of fiction and its value.

Curiously enough he does at one point partially accept a

Teaching Fiction in Schools

view of creativity which could be helpful, and thus undermine his approach. 'Is it that "the teacher conveys to young children—by his attitude to poetry and fiction—that he is able to receive and respect significant engagement with experience on an objective 'third ground' of imaginative effort with words"?' (Holbrook). Partly . . .' *But* poetry and fiction by themselves are not enough for Mr Dixon. There has to be real participation as well, so he proceeds: 'partly too in simple talk we may see the right attitude develop when the teacher, instead of capping pupils' stories or coming in as an observer might, lets his excitement at what the last speaker has said betray him into making his own contribution, telling as one of the group how perhaps he watched a huddle of ducklings bob over the ripples on the pond.' But of course, in the eyes of the Dartmouth Conference this too would be literature.

What Mr Dixon cannot understand is the need for 'third ground' if discoveries of a certain kind are to be effected. His fundamental concept is that of the growth of the child's world through language, and the means he recommends is the development of contact between the child's experience of others'. Thus, when discussing the study of literature, he asserts that 'the essential talk that springs from literature is talk about experience—as *we* know it, as he [the author] sees it.' But the 'third ground' of which Holbrook speaks belongs neither to our experience not to that of the author: it belongs to the experience of fiction, the 'world of entertainment'. We refer of course to entertainment as defined in Chapter 2, where the reader may also remember we instanced a game played by children, in which the people next door were supposed to be invaders from outer space. Such a game can be a shared experience, although the reality upon which it is based is purely conjectural. It is not difficult to see how children can learn things on 'this ground' which they could never learn anywhere else. And this is how unique lessons can be learnt from fiction.

Ends

The last point to make is that, since these lessons are indeed unique, they are not to be learnt by any other study. At the outset we stressed that they were not to be confused with the lessons of History or Geography. Our concluding stress is that they are no more to be confused with those of Theology or Psychology. What is profoundly questionable about some of the work of David Holbrook and, for example, Simon Stuart's otherwise sensitive and underrated *Say* (1969) is the way in which they reduce the labours of the imagination to the dignified indulgences of Fantasy. In these writers the *end* of literary study is mistaken. Most teachers will not require that they have Freudian (or other) insights into the members of their English classes: but even if these are, or may in special circumstances become, useful, they can only be so as guides to finding the right questions to ask. Questions to ask about what? Not about the pupil's problems, but about their experience of fiction.

SUBJECT INDEX

Collaboration of teacher and pupil, 35–6, 149
Comprehension
    dangers of concentration upon, 11–12, 14, 22–5
    example of its limitations, 22–3
    involves criticism, 14, 22, 24
    transcended, 50, 147
    uses of, 44
Concern
    activated by fiction, 28
    in *A Bear Called Paddington*, 41–2
    in *Daisy Miller*, 127–8, 131
    in *Daughters of the Vicar*, 112, 113
    in *The Dead*, 133–5, 142
    in *Goldilocks*, 20–1, 33
    in *Great Expectations*, 89–90
    in *Huckleberry Finn*, 71–7
    in *Pride and Prejudice*, 105–7
    in *A Simple Heart*, 145
    in *The Tower by the Sea*, 48
    in *Treasure Island*, 62–5
    need not be contemporary or social, 125–8
Conventions
    child's mastery of, 18, 32–3
    in *A Bear Called Paddington*, 40
Criticism
    and alertness, 126–7, 131
    boredom and disappointment, 15, 18, 43, 58, 79
    capacity for, 11–12, 16–17, 20
    comparisons, 40, 121

Subject Index

consciousness of imaginative process, 25, 31–3, 40
instruments require tactful use, 38
moral judgement and, 20
sense of implications, 54–5, 111, 126, 131
Ending, essentials of a good, 19–21, 33
Expectation, 19–20, 33
Fact
  Flaubert's sense of, 145
  relationship of fiction with, 12, 17–18, 25, 31, 82
Guidance
  offered by teacher, 17, 24, 29, 79, 126–7
  to approach Jane Austen, 98, 102–3, 107
  to avoid stock response, 113
  useless with jokes, 80
Humour
  of Charles Dickens, 80–2
  of Henry James, 131
  of Mark Twain, 73, 78
Imagination
  conscious use of, 32–3
  historical, 53–4, 103–4
  intrinsic value of, 25, 152
Integrated Studies
  incompatible with critical, 31–2, 148–9
  topics, 12
Interest
  illustrated from *Goldilocks*, 18–20
  peculiar, of fiction, 17–18
Irony
  and moral judgement, 100–1, 109
  and sarcasm, 99–100
  and sympathy, 23, 132, 135
  child's concept of, 35–7
  of linguistic register, 71–2, 76, 147
  of narrator, 23, 61–2, 71, 76–7, 90–1, 128
Method, systematic, useless, 29
Myth, 28, 54
Names, significance of fictitious, 18, 84 (footnote), 129, 137, 140, 143
Pattern
  of *Dawn Wind*, 56
  of *The Dead*, 136–41
  of *Great Expectations*, 84–90
Plot, distinguished from story, 24

Subject Index

Psychology
    in the classroom, 153
    of Dickens' characters, 82–3, 86
    of fictitious characters, 23–4
    of Long John Silver, 66–8
Questions to elicit awareness of
    distance, 32–3, 40, 43, 50–1, 90–1, 93–4, 114, 130
    irony, 35–7, 62, 75–7, 90–1, 99–100
    narrative trend, 33–4, 44, 46, 56–7
    sympathetic flow, 37–8, 46–7, 50–1, 60–2, 78, 100
    verbal detail, 34–5, 36, 45, 50–1, 55, 59, 71–2, 88, 94–5, 98, 104, 107, 109, 111–12, 113, 115, 116, 118, 129, 130, 133, 136, 137, 140
Reading
    again, 113, 131, 136
    aloud, 35–6
Realism
    and truth, 20
    in Charles Dickens, 82–3
    in Flaubert, 145
    of Jane Austen, 102–3
    of De Jong, 49
    symbolic in D. H. Lawrence, 111; and James Joyce, 132, 137
Relationship
    of characters in *Great Expectations*, 83–4
    of Elizabeth Bennet and Mr Darcy, 28, 102
    of Huckleberry Finn and Tom, 78–9
    of Jim Hawkins with other characters, 64–70
    vital v. dutiful in *Daughters of the Vicar*, 116–21
Sentimentality, 72, 96, 143–4
Sociological interest
    distinguished from literary, 125–6, 151
    of *Daughters of the Vicar*, 113
    of *Great Expectations*, 84, 93–4
    of *Huckleberry Finn*, 71
    of *A Simple Heart*, 144
    of *Treasure Island*, 65
Suspense
    distinguished from curiosity, 27–8
    in *A Bear Called Paddington*, 46
    in *Goldilocks*, 19, 33
    in *Treasure Island*, 66
Symbolism
    in *Daughters of the Vicar*, 111, 123–4

Subject Index

  in *Great Expectations*, 87–9, 94
  in *The Dead*, 137–41
Sympathy
  and irony, 23, 37, 47, 128–30, 133–5
  and morality, 48, 73–5, 78, 116–17
  division of, 47, 49–50, 59–60, 128
  for fictitious characters, 24–6, 37–8, 46–7, 68–70, 97–8, 101–2
Theme, 112 (see also Concern)
Trigger, classroom use of literature as a, 17
Value judgements
  complexity of, 50
  implicit v. explicit, 20–1, 74, 91–2, 131
Wit, 98–100
Written Work, 38

INDEX OF AUTHORS

Austen, Jane, 97–110

Baldwick, Robert, 143
Barstow, Stan, 125
Bolt, Sydney, 17
Bond, Michael, 39–47
Braine, John, 125
Brown, Douglas, 71, 142

Coleridge, S. T., 29
Conrad, Joseph, 49, 142
Crompton, Richmael, 41

De Jong, Meindert, 48–52, 125
De Vries, Peter, 146
Dickens, Charles, 97–110, 144
Dixon, John, 150–2

Eliot, George, 83, 86, 136

Flaubert, Gustave, 142–7

Golding, William, 125

Hart, Bret, 71
Holbrook, David, 152, 153

James, Henry, 16, 127–31, 143
Johnson, Samuel, 110, 148
Jonson, Ben, 71
Joyce, James, 131–42, 143

Lawrence, D. H., 26, 111–24, 137
Leavis, F. R., 78, 80, 148

Santayana, George, 82
Shakespeare, William, 32, 80, 123
Shaw, G. B., 91–2
Sidnell, M. J., 79
Sillitoe, Alan, 125
Southey, Robert, 20–1
Stevens, Wallace, 136
Stevenson, R. L., 59–70
Stewart, Simon, 153
Summerfield, Geoffrey, 12, 14
Sutcliffe, Rosemary, 53–8
Swift, Jonathan, 71, 72, 79

Walsh, J. H., 11, 13–16, 22–3
Whitehead, Frank, 11, 13–17
Whitehead, Robert, 31
Wilde, Oscar, 99
Wordsworth, William, 31